3

Network

GET CONNECTED

Tom Hutchinson
Kristin Sherman

OXFORD
UNIVERSITY PRESS

OXFORD
UNIVERSITY PRESS

198 Madison Avenue
New York, NY 10016 USA

Great Clarendon Street, Oxford, OX2 6DP, United Kingdom

Oxford University Press is a department of the University of Oxford.
It furthers the University's objective of excellence in research, scholarship,
and education by publishing worldwide. Oxford is a registered trademark of
Oxford University Press in the UK and in certain other countries

© Oxford University Press 2012

The moral rights of the author have been asserted

First published in 2012

2016 2015 2014 2013 2012

10 9 8 7 6 5 4 3 2 1

No unauthorized photocopying

General Manager: Laura Pearson
Executive Publishing Manager: Erik Gundersen
Managing Editor: Louisa van Houten
Associate Editor: Tristan Child
Director, ADP: Susan Sanguily
Design Manager: Lisa Donovan
Designers: Jessica Balaschak
Electronic Production Manager: Julie Armstrong
Production Artists: Julie Sussman-Perez
Image Manager: Trisha Masterson
Image Editor: Liaht Pashayan
Production Coordinator: Chris Espejo

ISBN: 978 0 19 467155 2 WORKBOOK

Printed in China

This book is printed on paper from certified and well-managed sources

ACKNOWLEDGEMENTS

Cover Design: Molly K. Scanlon

Illustrations by: Cyrus Deboo: pg. 6, 14, 28, 42, 68, 69, 76; James Fletcher: pg. 8, 26; Chris Pavely: pg. 61; Roger Penwill: pg. 3, 25, 32, 56, 79, 81.

We would also like to thank the following for permission to reproduce the following photographs. Cover photos: Cover photos: AM-STUDiO/shutterstock.com, olly/shutterstock.com, Losevsky Pavel/shutterstock.com, koh sze kiat/shutterstock.com, Mika Heittola/shutterstock.com, Konstantin Sutyagin/shutterstock.com, Artem Zhushman/shutterstock.com, ilolab/shutterstock.com, Jason Stitt/shutterstock.com, Nickolya/shutterstock.com, shock/shutterstock.com, Shvaygert Ekaterina/shutterstock.com, AJP/shutterstock.com, BestPhotoStudio/shutterstock.com, Yuri Arcurs/shutterstock.com, JonMilnes/shutterstock.com, qingqing/shutterstock.com, Goodluz/shutterstock.com, Matthew Williams-Ellis/shutterstock.com, BestPhotoStudio/shutterstock.com, Christian Bertrand/Shutterstock.com. Pg. 12 karamysh/shutterstock.com; pg. 16 Somos/OUP; pg. 19 (Christie) Moodboard/OUP, (Sarah) Jack Hollingsworth/OUP, (John) Photodisc/OUP; pg. 22 OLIVIER JOBARD/epa/Corbis; pg. 37 (Racer) incamerastock/Alamy, (Words) 1MoreCreative/istockphoto.com, (Warcraft) LiPo Ching/MCT/Newscom; pg. 48 Pictorial Press Ltd/Alamy; pg. 55 Blend_Images/istockphoto.com; pg. 58 wavebreakmedia ltd/shutterstock.com; pg. 62 BLOOMimage/Gett Images; pg. 74 (Roberto) Cusp/SuperStock, (Julia) Blend Images/shutterstock.com; pg. 75 (a) lillisphotography/istockphoto.com, (b) David M. Albrecht/shutterstock.com, (c) James R. Martin/shutterstock.com, (d) Yulia_B/shutterstock.com; pg. 77 (baggage) Garry Black/Masterfile, (taxi) Corbis Bridge/Alamy, (car) Tommaso79/shutterstock.com, (traffic) Amy Tseng/shutterstock.com, (delay) Péter Gudella/shutterstock.com; pg. 78 Mike Liu/Shutterstock.com; pg. 80 (man 1) Image Source/OUP, (woman 1) Alexander Raths/shutterstock.com, (man 2) EDHAR/shutterstock.com, (woman 2) Jack Hollingsworth/Getty Images *Additional photography provided by:* Ken Karp, Sergej Khakimullin/shutterstock.com, Anna Maniowska/istockphoto.com, Rubberball/istockphoto.com, peter zelei/istockphoto.com, Tom Young/istockphoto.com, Supri Suharjoto/shutterstock.com, Tom Wang/shutterstock.com, Kurhan/shutterstock.com, Felix Mizioznikov/shutterstock.com, Kateryna Upit/shutterstock.co, Marko Tomicic/shutterstock.com, James Peragine/shutterstock.com, Christopher Oates/shutterstock.com, AISPIX/shutterstock.com, Matthew Williams-Ellis/shutterstock.com, Peter Kirillov/shutterstock.com, Andrey Arkusha/shutterstock.com.

Contents

Unit

Let's introduce ourselves.

A VOCABULARY: Personal information

1 Circle the correct words.

Hello. My name's Ken Tashita. I'm an electrician, but I'm (**unemployed**) / out of employed now.

I'm looking for a job. I'm not __marry / **married**__, but I have a fiancée. We're __**engaged** / engage__,

but we want to wait to get married for a while. My fiancée's name is Miki, and she is

__**self-employed** / own-employed__. She owns her own __work / **business**__, and she runs it from an

office in her home. My roommate, Jake, is a __**manager** / management__ at a bank.

He supervises ten other people. I live near my mother. She __retiree / **retired**__ three years ago.

She is also a __widow / **widowed**__. Miki and I often check on her to make sure she is OK.

2 Complete the sentences about the people in Activity 1.

1. Ken isn't working. He's __unemployed__.

2. Ken and Miki plan to get married. They are _____.

3. At the moment, Miki is Ken's _____.

4. Ken's mother stopped working three years ago. She's _____.

5. Ken's father died. His mother is a _____.

6. Jake supervises other people at work. He's a _____.

7. Miki doesn't work for anyone else. She's _____.

3 Complete the chart with information about you.

Full name:	
Age:	
Street address:	
City:	
Job:	
Employer:	
Place of study:	
Marital status:	

B GRAMMAR: Present simple and present continuous

1 Rewrite the sentences with the new subject.

1. I live in a big city. He _____ lives in a big city _____.

2. I don't like traveling to work. She _____.

3. I usually wash the car on Sunday. He _____.

4. I don't drive to work. She _____.

2 What are the people doing? Write two sentences about each picture.

1. he / swim / run
   _____ He's swimming _____.
   _____ He isn't running _____.

3. they / eat / watch TV
   _____.
   _____.

2. she / write a letter /
   read a book
   _____.
   _____.

4. I / shop / drive
   _____.
   _____.

3 Complete the story. Use the present simple or present continuous form of the verbs.

I ____live____ (live) in a small apartment near downtown. However, I _____ (not stay)
1   2

there this week. I _____ (stay) with my brother for a few days. I _____ (work) near my
3   4

home, so I usually _____ (walk) to my office, but this week I _____ (take) the bus
5   6

because my brother _____ (not live) near my work. However, I _____ (enjoy) the week.
7   8

I _____ (not see) my brother very often, and we always _____ (have) a good time together.
9   10

4 Complete the conversation. Use the correct form of the verbs.

A: I'm ____looking for____ (look for) my cell phone. I _____ (want) to call Louise.
1   2

B: You _____ (not need) to do that. I _____ (think) she's over there.
3   4

Yes, she is. She _____ (talk) to Pedro at the moment.
5

A: OK, but I still _____ (need) my cell phone. Oh, I _____ (know).
6   7

It's in the car. I _____ (go) to get it now.
8

B: But Louise _____ (come) over here now.
9

A: I can talk to her later. I _____ (not like) leaving my phone in the car.
10

C READING AND WRITING: Reasons for doing something

1 Read the Web page. What kind of class is this? Write the correct subject below.

Our _____ class.

T.J.   11/11   6:15 p.m.
Hello. It was great to meet everyone in class today. Please tell everyone a little about why you are taking this class.

Mario   11/11   7:10 p.m.
Hi. My name is Mario Garcia. I'm retired so I have a lot of free time. My wife used to do all the cooking, but now I want to help her. We're eating less meat and more vegetables because they are healthier, so I'm excited to learn more about that. That's why I'm taking this class.

Casey   11/11   7:32 p.m.
Hi! I'm excited to meet everyone. I'm taking this class because I'm a mother of two young children. I want them to eat more vegetables. They don't want to. I want to learn how to cook vegetarian food for my kids.

Max   11/11   9:47 p.m.
OK, so I'm a great cook, but I cook mainly meat and potatoes. I know it's time to change my habits. I don't eat very healthy foods. I eat fast food a lot. In fact, I'm having a delicious pizza right now! I love pizza. Anyway, I'm engaged to a woman who always eats healthy foods. I want to show her that I can cook healthy foods, too, so we can cook together.

Eva   11/12   8:03 a.m.
I'm Evaline, but please call me Eva. I'm taking this class because I'm engaged to a vegetarian. I never really thought about eating this way before. I want to learn about, it and surprise my fiancé. Also, I'm unemployed at the moment, so I have some free time. I'm looking forward to getting to know everyone!

2 Match each person with the correct reason.

_____ 1. T.J.

_____ 2. Mario

_____ 3. Casey

_____ 4. Max

_____ 5. Eva

a. wants her children to eat more vegetables.

b. wants to impress her fiancé.

c. wants to change his habits and start eating healthier.

d. is retired and wants to cook more with his wife.

e. is the teacher.

3 Who do you think said each sentence? Write the correct name.

1. _____ Come on, honey. Let's go get a pizza. Just this one time.

2. _____ Come over after work. I have a surprise for you tonight.

3. _____ You go put your feet up, dear. I'm cooking dinner for you tonight.

4. _____ Come on, everyone. It's dinnertime. I made something new for you tonight.

5. _____ I'm excited to share my love of cooking with you.

D EVERYDAY EXPRESSIONS: Future arrangements

1 Complete Sarah Ramiro's summary. Use the words in the boxes.

working	children	girlfriend	son	wants	Australia

Cindy and Ryan Gaskell own a cafe called Cozy Cup. They have two _____.
1

Their daughter, Melanie, is a student, and their _____, Russell,
2

is looking for a job. Wiping the tables in this picture is Jordan Morris.

Jordan's from _____. He's _____ in the cafe
3   4

now, but he really _____ to be an actor. He's waiting for
5

his _____, Lucy. Lucy Patterson is a copywriter. She
6

_____ in an advertising agency.
7

works	walking	sales manager	dating	student

In this picture, Lucy is _____ into the cafe
8

with Matt Morris and Peter Colombo. Peter and I are

_____. Peter is a _____. I'm
9   10

from Brazil. I'm a _____.
11

2 Complete the conversations. Use the words in parentheses.

1. **A:** _____ Are you doing _____ anything this evening? (you / do)

   B: Yes, I am. _____ I'm going _____ to the movies. (I / go)

2. **A:** _____ this weekend? (Jordan / work)

   B: No, I think _____ Lucy's parents. (he / visit)

3. **A:** When _____? (they / leave)

   B: _____ down on Saturday morning. (they / drive)

4. **A:** What _____ tomorrow? (Peter and Sarah / do)

   B: _____ at some houses. (they / look)

UNIT 2 Things happen.

A VOCABULARY: Expressions with *get*

1 Complete the sentences. Use the expressions in the box with *getting* or *get*.

get hungry	get a text	~~get lost~~	get ready	get home	get locked out

1. I wish we had a map. I don't know where we are. I think we are _____ getting lost _____.

2. We eat dinner at 6:00. The children _____ around then every evening.

3. What sound does your cell phone make when you _____ ?

4. Alyssa's working late tonight. She's _____ for her presentation tomorrow.

5. If you don't remember your key, you will _____ of your apartment.

6. If I take the number seven bus, I _____ at around 5:30.

2 Complete the sentences. Use the expressions in the box in the past simple.

get angry	~~get quiet~~	get bigger	get cold	get worse	get married

1. It was too noisy to work, but then it _____ got quiet _____ after the children went to sleep.

2. You should take a jacket with you. It _____ last night.

3. Congratulations! I heard you _____ last month!

4. The bump on his head _____ while he was sleeping.

5. Megan and Andrea lived together last year but they were terrible roommates. They often _____ with each other.

6. The storm wasn't too bad in the morning, but it _____ during the day.

3 What's happening in the pictures? Complete the sentences. Use the words in the box with *getting*.

taller	worse	closer	~~louder~~

1. _The TV's getting_ _louder_ .

2. _The car_ _____ .

3. _The weather_ _____ .

4. _John_ _____ .

6

B GRAMMAR: Present perfect with *for* and *since*

1 Complete the chart. Use *have* or *has* and *for* or *since*.

	have or *has*	Past participle	*for* or *since*	Time
I You We They	_____	been a student here	_____	six months. one year. a short time.
He She	_____	known her	_____	last year. December.

2 Put the expressions in the correct column.

2003	five minutes	yesterday	three weeks
four hours	11:30	Monday	nearly a month

for + a period of time	*since* + a point in time
_____	_____
_____	_____
_____	_____
_____	_____

3 Circle the correct answers.

1. I *have / has* lived in this apartment *for / since* May.

2. Sheila and Andre *have been / has be* married *for / since* a long time.

3. *They've / They has* been on the bus *for / since* 2:30.

4. Jon has *live / lived* in Mexico *for / since* one year.

5. Marcus *haven't / hasn't* had a job *for / since* 2009.

4 Make *How long ...* questions with each of the statements in Activity 3.

1. _____

2. _____

3. _____

4. _____

5. _____

C READING AND WRITING: A series of events

1 Read the story. Why did Marie get annoyed in the first version?
What happened in the second version?

Marie's Bad Day

Marie got an e-mail on Monday morning from a design studio. It said, "I'm sorry, but we can't send your posters today. The designer got sick, and hasn't been able to finish them." When she read it, Marie got very annoyed. Her boss needed the posters for an important meeting that morning. She turned around angrily. Unfortunately, there was a glass of water on the desk and she knocked it over with her arm. The glass fell on the floor and broke.

When Marie's secretary, Fatima, heard the noise, she came into the office. "Did you have to put that glass near the edge of the desk?" Marie shouted at her. "I'm sorry," said Fatima, and she bent down to pick up the pieces of glass. Because she was upset, she picked one piece up too quickly and cut her hand badly.

Marie had to take her to the hospital, but because she was in a hurry, she forgot to tell her boss about the posters. They were at the hospital for a long time, and afterwards Fatima had to go home. When Marie got back to work, her boss was annoyed because he didn't know about the posters before the meeting. It was a bad start to the week.

Did it have to be a bad start? No, it didn't. In a second version of the story, Marie didn't get annoyed about the e-mail. She reacted calmly. She called her boss. He said, "OK. These things happen. We'll move the meeting to next week." Marie sat back in her chair, drank her glass of water, and had a good day.

2 Complete the sentences with the correct subject.

Marie	Her boss	Fatima	The designer

1. _____Fatima_____ cut her hand.   3. _____ got sick.

2. _____ knocked over the glass.   4. _____ needed the posters.

3 Complete the sentences about Marie. Use *had to* and the verbs in the box.

apologize	buy	type	~~take~~

1. She _____had to take_____ Fatima to the hospital.

2. She _____ some flowers for her.

3. She _____ to her boss.

4. She _____ her own reports.

D EVERYDAY EXPRESSIONS: Possessions

1 Complete the chart.

Possessive adjectives	Possessive pronouns
1. This is my cell phone.	It's _____mine_____.
2. Is this _____ book?	Is this yours?
3. They're his glasses.	They're _____.
4. That's _____ bike.	That bike is hers.
5. These are our seats.	These seats are _____.
6. That's _____ car.	It's theirs.

2 Complete the conversations. Use the words in the boxes.

hers	belong	her (x2)	~~whose~~	his

A: _____Whose_____ keys are these?
1

B: I think they _____ to Tina. She usually sits there.
2

A: No, they aren't _____. This isn't _____ car key.
3   4

B: Well, _____ boyfriend drives that kind of car. They're probably
5

_____.
6

mine	to	belongs	does	yours	my

A: Who _____ that briefcase belong _____?
1   2

Is it _____?
3

B: No, it isn't _____. _____ briefcase is here.
4   5

A: Oh, I know. It _____ to Martin.
6

our (x2)	doesn't	belong	ours	theirs	whose

A: _____ cat is that? Does it _____ to _____
1   2   3

new neighbors?

B: No, it _____. That cat's a lot bigger than _____.
4   5

A: Well, it certainly isn't _____, so why is it in _____ yard?
6   7

UNIT 3 Buildings everywhere!

A VOCABULARY: Describing housing

1 Match the opposites.

_____ 1. spacious   a. quiet

_____ 2. dark   b. on the ground floor

_____ 3. noisy   c. small

_____ 4. not near anything   d. convenient

_____ 5. on the top floor   e. light

2 Complete the text with the words in the box.

first floor	location	building	~~apartment~~	spacious
furniture	convenient	light	empty	

Bill has just moved into a new ___apartment___ . It's on the _____. Bill's
                                    1   2

apartment is very small. There are only three rooms. The rooms aren't very _____,
         3

but he doesn't mind because he doesn't have much _____. The apartment has very
         4

big windows, so it is nice and _____. Bill likes that a lot. Also, it's in a good
         5

_____. There are lots of stores around, and it's close to public transportation. It's
    6

very _____ for a student without a car like Bill. There are four apartments in Bill's
       7

_____. There's a young family living upstairs and another student living next door.
    8

The fourth apartment is _____.
         9

3 Write about the place where you live. Circle the correct words and complete the sentences.

I live in _a/an_ _____. I _own / rent_ the _____. It's _furnished /
unfurnished_ and it has _____ rooms—a _____,
_____, and _____. The rooms are _____. The
house / apartment has _____ and _____, but it doesn't have
_____. I live with _____. I _like / don't_ like the place because it's
_____ and it's _____.

GRAMMAR: Articles

1 Complete the rules. Choose from the words in parentheses.

The indefinite article: *(the/a/an)*
We use *a/an* with a _____ noun. *(singular/plural)*
We use *a/an* for something that is _____ . *(specific/not specific)*
I'm going to a concert. I like concerts.

2 Write *the* in the correct place in each sentence.

1. My apartment is on ^the^ tenth floor.

2. This is best online bulletin board.

3. My office is near police station.

4. This is third house that we've looked at.

3 Complete the story with *a, an,* or *the.*

Lauren is looking at ___*a*___ new apartment today. It's on _____ second floor of
                          1   2

_____ old house. _____ landlord is showing her around. He lives on _____ first floor.
      3   4   5

_____ apartment has four rooms: a kitchen, _____ bathroom, _____ bedroom, and
      6   7   8

_____ living room. _____ bedroom is small, but _____ living room is very spacious.
      9   10   11

_____ apartment is furnished, so there's _____ bed and _____ dresser in _____
      12   13   14   15

bedroom. There's _____ sofa, _____ armchair and _____ table with four chairs in
                        16   17   18

_____ living room. _____ house is near downtown, and is in one of _____ most
      19   20   21

expensive areas, so Lauren will need _____ roommate to share _____ rent.
                                              22   23

4 Write *a, an,* or *the* where necessary in the conversations.

1. **A:** We went to ^a^ concert at ^the^ theater yesterday.

   B: Was concert good?

   A: Yes, it was best concert I've ever seen. Orchestra was great.

2. **A:** Excuse me. Is there ATM near here?

   B: Yes, there's ATM on first floor next to elevator.

3. **A:** There's new supermarket near gym.

   B: Is supermarket good?

   A: Yes, and it's biggest in area.

C READING AND WRITING: Vacation ideas

1 **Read the article. What does House Swapping mean?**

House Swapping

Do you like to travel but don't like spending a lot of money on hotels? Do you live in a nice location? Is it a location that people like to visit? If so, you should try House Swapping. House Swapping is an organization that helps people swap houses with other people for their vacations. On the House Swapping website you will find listings of apartments and houses in places all over the world. Post your house. Describe your house and its location. How many bedrooms does it have? (Remember, no house or apartment is too small!) How close to public transportation is it? What is nearby? Why would anyone want to stay in your house? What dates will you be away? After you post your house, surf the website for a house in a location where you want to go. You can use our website for locations all around the world. You can find listings for houses that are available for short or long periods of time, although the minimum amount of time is usually a week. Listings in locations without good public transportation often provide the use of a car, too. Do you have a pet? You can swap houses with someone else who has a pet. You take care of your House Swappers' pet while they take care of yours. You can travel to wonderful locations and stay in nice houses without breaking the bank. We currently have over 10,000 listings. To make a swap, join the site. All you need to do is pay the small membership fee of $125 which is good for one year. Get in touch with a House Swapper for your next vacation. You won't regret it!

2 **Match the words or phrases from the article above with words or phrases with a similar meaning.**

_____ 1. swap	a. houses on the website
_____ 2. listings	b. can be used for
_____ 3. post your house	c. buses, trains, and subways
_____ 4. public transportation	d. trade
_____ 5. minimum	e. the shortest amount of time
_____ 6. good for	f. put a description of your home on the website

3 **Mark the statements about House Swapping true (T) or false (F)?**

1. _____ You can use the House Swapping website for free.

2. _____ You need to have a house to house swap.

3. _____ You can house swap with an apartment or a house.

4. _____ All the houses on the website are large.

5. _____ If you have a pet, you cannot house swap.

6. _____ There are houses on the website from all over the world.

7. _____ Only houses near public transportation can be posted on the website.

8. _____ The House Swapping website is only for people going on long vacations.

D EVERYDAY EXPRESSIONS: Checking into a hotel

1 Complete the expressions. Use the words in the box.

check	is served	any help	luggage
is correct	non-smoking	reservation	a double room

1. Is that a _____ room?

2. Breakfast _____ until 10:00.

3. We'd like _____ for six nights, please.

4. Could you _____ that all the information _____, please?

5. Do you have a _____?

6. Do you need _____ with your _____?

2 Complete the conversation between the receptionist (R) and a guest (G). Use the words and phrases from Activity 1.

R: Good evening. Do you have a _____₁?

G: Yes, my last name is Jesperson.

R: Just one moment, please. Here it is. _____₂ for three nights?

G: Yes, that's correct. And we'd like a _____₃ room, please.

R: There's no smoking anywhere in the hotel, actually.

G: Great! Is breakfast included?

R: Yes, it is. Breakfast _____₄ until 9:00. Can I see your credit card?

G: Yes, here you are.

R: Thank you. Here's your card. And could you _____₅ that all the information on this form _____₆ and sign it?

G: It's all correct. Here you are. Do you have any extra toothbrushes? I forgot mine.

R: Certainly. Here's your key. Do you need _____₇ with your _____₈?

G: No, thank you.

3 Circle the correct sentences.

1. a. All our rooms are non-smoking.

   b. All our rooms are not smoking.

2. a. Do you have a reservation?

   b. Do you have the reservation?

3. a. Could you sign at the form, please?

   b. Could you sign the form, please?

4. a. Breakfast is served at 6:00 to 9:30.

   b. Breakfast is served from 6:00 to 9:30.

UNIT 4 Seeing old friends

A VOCABULARY: Phrasal verbs

1 Label the pictures. Choose from the phrasal verbs in the box.

run into	catch up	throw out	take off	turn up	~~turn down~~

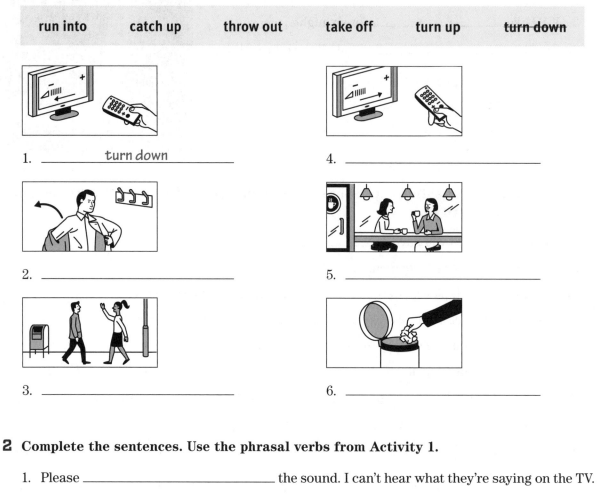

1. _____turn down_____

4. _____

2. _____

5. _____

3. _____

6. _____

2 Complete the sentences. Use the phrasal verbs from Activity 1.

1. Please _____ the sound. I can't hear what they're saying on the TV.

2. I don't _____ receipts. I always save them.

3. Aren't you hot? Why don't you _____ your sweater?

4. You should _____ your MP3 player. It's not good for your ears!

5. It's so good to see you. Let's get together and _____ over coffee soon.

6. I always _____ old friends when I go to visit my parents.

3 Complete the statements about you.

1. The last old friend I ran into was _____ .

2. The one friend I always like catching up with is _____ .

3. The one thing I never throw out is _____ .

4. When I'm at home I always take off _____ .

5. I'm always asking _____ to turn up/turn down the music.

B GRAMMAR: Separable and inseparable phrasal verbs

1 Complete the chart. Choose from the words in the box.

~~look up~~	separable	next to	take out	turn up
get off	object	figure out	get over	particles (x2)

Explanation	Examples	
1. Phrasal verbs are verbs + _____ such as *in, on, off, up, over, out, up,* and *down*.	*verb* go	*particle* out
2. _____ phrasal verbs are verbs that can have an _____ between them and their particles.	<u>look up</u> _____ _____ _____	
3. Inseparable phrasal verbs are verbs that have to be _____ their _____ .	_____ _____	

2 Complete the sentences. Use the phrasal verbs in the chart above.

1. Can you help me? I can't _____<u>figure out</u>_____ this puzzle.

2. Eddie broke up with his girlfriend last year and he's still very sad. He can't seem to _____ her.

3. The bus driver forgot to tell Joe what bus stop to _____ at, so he got lost.

4. Jody is old enough now to _____ the recycling herself.

5. Our teacher told us to _____ all the new words in our dictionaries.

6. It's very cold in this house. Let's _____ the heat.

3 Find the sentences in Activity 2 with separable phrasal verbs. Rewrite them in another way.

<u>Can you help me? I can't figure this puzzle out.</u>

_____

_____

_____

4 Write the particles in parentheses in the two possible places they can go in the sentences.
1. Let's throw﹀the newspapers﹀. We have too many. (out) *[out written above both carets]*

2. Can you turn the music, please? It's too loud. (down)

3. Would you like to take your shoes? They look very uncomfortable. (off)

4. Jonah's in the dressing room trying some clothes at the moment. (on)

1 **Read the story. When did Sandra graduate from university? Where does she live now?**

Graduate Updates

Sandra Kneale

    I graduated 12 years ago. In the first two years after school, I tried a lot of different jobs. I couldn't figure out what I wanted to do. First, I worked in a lawyer's office for six months. Then in a clothing store. I tried a few other places too, but I didn't like any of the jobs. Finally, I got a job as a real estate agent for a company in Tampa, Florida. I enjoyed looking at houses and taking people to see them. I really liked the job, and met some very interesting people, too. I worked there for four years, but I really wanted to start my own company and be my own boss. However, there was a lot of competition. Many people were going into real estate at that time. I got my chance when I took some time off to go to Dubai to visit some friends. I was only there for ten days, but while I was there, I met my future husband, Sami. He's from Finland, and he works in the oil industry. Sami showed me around Dubai, and it was amazing. They were building thousands of houses and apartments. I thought this was the place for my new company. I moved to Dubai to be with Sami and started my own real estate agency. We got married a year later, and now we have two children—a boy and a girl. I've been here for six years, and the company is doing very well. It's been a little more difficult since the children were born, but it's still great. I think my move here was the best decision that I've ever made.

2 **Mark the statements true (T) or false (F)?**

_____ 1. Sandra didn't know which job she wanted after she graduated.

_____ 2. She didn't like taking people to see houses.

_____ 3. There were a lot of real estate agencies in Florida.

_____ 4. Sandra met her husband on a visit to Dubai.

_____ 5. Sandra has her own company now.

_____ 6. She's been married for ten years.

3 **Match the two parts of the sentences.**

_____ 1. Sandra graduated   a. for ten days.

_____ 2. She worked in a lawyer's office   b. for six months.

_____ 3. She sold houses in Tampa   c. for six years.

_____ 4. She went to Dubai   d. 12 years ago.

_____ 5. She's lived in Dubai   e. for five years.

_____ 6. She's been married   f. for four years.

D EVERYDAY EXPRESSIONS: Recognizing people

1 Number the parts of the story in the correct order.

_____ a. Felton tells Jordan that his secretary, Violet, will be in touch in the next few days. Jordan doesn't understand.

_____ b. Felton asks Jordan to read something. It's the part of Red Mason in a soap opera. Jordan doesn't understand, but he reads the part.

_____ c. Felton explains that he's the producer of a new soap opera called "Downtown Hospital," and he's auditioning actors. He thinks Jordan came for an audition.

_____ d. Felton asks his name and says that Jordan looks familiar. He recognizes him from a commercial.

_____ e. Jordan says he didn't know anything about the auditions. He was there to drop off some food.

__1__ f. Jordan goes to an office. There's nobody at the reception desk, so he knocks on the door of Felton Windrush's office.

_____ g. Felton says that Jordan read the part very well and he's happy to hear that Jordan is from Australia.

2 Find the mistakes. Rewrite the expressions correctly.

1. You look family. _____You look familiar._____

2. I know face. _____

3. I thought I recognized. _____

4. I never forget the face. _____

5. I seen her before. _____

3 Complete the conversation. Use the expressions from Activity 2.

A: Who's that man over there? I'm sure _____I've seen_____ him _____before_____, and I
                                            1   2

never _____.
            3

B: Why don't you go and ask him?

A: OK. Excuse me. You _____. Have I seen you before?
                              4

C: I don't think so.

A: But I know _____.
                      5

C: Well, I'm Jack Massey.

A: Oh, of course. You read the local news on TV. I thought _____.
                                                                  6

GET CONNECTED

Protecting your privacy online

Social networking can be a great way to communicate and share information with old and new friends and co-workers. However, it's important to remember that social networks are public. Anyone who has access to your personal information may use that information in a dangerous way. Also, clicking on certain links on these sites can spread viruses to your computer. So how can you protect yourself?

1. Don't post your address or information about your daily schedule.

2. Don't post information that you don't want everyone to see. Your employer or future employers may see this information.

3. Be careful when people you don't know want to connect with you. Make sure they know someone that you know. Don't connect with someone you are not sure about.

4. Most sites ask you to answer a question before they send you a password-reminder e-mail. These can be questions like, "What was the name of your first pet?" or "Where were you born?" Hackers look for the answers to these questions so they can take over your profile. Make up your own security question if you can.

5. Don't click on links that you're not sure about. Sometimes it looks like a friend posted a video or a link to a website. However, the link really takes you to a website with advertisements or puts a virus onto your computer. If you are not sure that a link is real, ask the friend who posted it.

GET Started

1 Look at social networking website A on page 19. Identify what is wrong with each post.

Christie   _____

Sarah   _____

John   _____

2 Look at the profile information on social networking website B. What is wrong with the profile?

_____

_____

▶▶▶ What's happening now?

Christie Gill

I just got an amazing deal! Click this link to find out more! http://xir.tg.ffo3_mm

Sarah Lopez

I'm going to Ken's Gym at 3:00 to work out. Then I'm going to City Pizza for dinner with some friends.

John Hong

My boss is making me so mad! I want to quit my job!

Your Profile

Name	Christie Gill
Location	Mexico City, Mexico
Hometown	Boston, Massachusetts
Contact Info	617-555-0983; christiegg@fremail.com

GET Together

GET To It!

3 Work with a partner. Look again at the tips about how to protect your privacy online on page 18. Have you ever done any of the things that the tips tell you not to do? Explain.

4 Write four security questions that you can use on social networks and other websites that require passwords. Don't write the answers!

1. _____

2. _____

3. _____

4. _____

> > > > > **Now I can...** protect my privacy online.

☐ Not at all ☐ Well ☐ Very well

Take it online

Change your social networking information to be more private.

Congratulations!

A VOCABULARY: Achievements

1 Match the two parts of the phrases.

_____ 1. win an   a. good grades

_____ 2. write a   b. promotion

_____ 3. get   c. award

_____ 4. climb a   d. marathon

_____ 5. run a   e. mountain

_____ 6. get a   f. book

2 Complete the sentences. Use the phrases from Activity 1. Put them in the present perfect or past simple.

1. Ray and Phil needed a challenge so they _____*climbed a mountain*_____ last year.

2. I run a few miles every day, but I've never _____.

3. Joshua went out to celebrate after he _____ at work.

4. Phoebe is very proud because she _____ for her work with homeless people.

5. I baked my daughter a cake because she _____ this semester.

6. Jorge has _____ about World War I. I hear that it is very interesting.

3 Complete the statements about you. Use the phrases from Activities 1 and 2.

1. I have never _____.

2. Once, I _____.

3. I have a friend who _____.

4. I have always / never wanted to _____.

5. I don't think I will ever _____.

6. I know someone who has _____.

4 Write a statement about something you have achieved in each time period.

1. Yesterday: _____.

2. Last week: _____.

3. Last month: _____.

4. This year: _____.

5. In the last ten years: _____.

B GRAMMAR: Present perfect and past simple

1 Complete the chart with the words in the box.

We	hasn't	It	They	have	She	didn't	You	yet

Present perfect: statements		
I, _____, _____, _____	_____ haven't	been absent two times. been absent _____.
He, _____, _____	has _____	gotten lost five times. gotten lost yet.
Past simple: statements		
I, We, He, She, You, They	found _____ find	an apartment to rent yesterday.

2 Complete the sentences. Use the verbs in parentheses in the present perfect or past simple.

1. He _'s climbed_____ many mountains in Switzerland. (climb)

2. The mail _____ at 10:00. (arrive)

3. We _____ lunch at 1:00 yesterday. (eat)

4. I _____ her name last class. (forget)

5. They _____ five miles yesterday morning. (run)

3 Make the sentences in Activity 2 negative.

1. _____.

2. _____.

3. _____.

4. _____.

5. _____.

4 Complete the sentences. Use the correct tense.

1. Martin can't go hiking with us. He _____ (break) his leg last week. He
   _____ (fall off) a horse. He _____ (have) two riding accidents this year.

2. I _____ (fill out) the form yesterday, so I can send it now. I _____
   (download) it from the Internet. I _____ (never do) that before.

3. I can't call you. I _____ (lose) my cell phone yesterday. I _____
   (leave) it on the bus. I _____ (never lose) anything before.

C **READING AND WRITING:** Amazing accomplishments

1 Read the article. Circle the buildings that Felix has jumped off.

1. The Petronas Towers
2. The Turning Torso
3. The Empire State Building
4. Canary Wharf
5. Taipei 101
6. The Eiffel Tower

BASE jumper

Felix Baumgartner loves skyscrapers, but he doesn't just like taking photographs of them. He likes jumping off them! Felix is a BASE jumper. That means he has jumped from four kinds of high places—buildings, antennae (TV towers), spans (bridges) and the earth (cliffs and mountains).

Fearless Felix, as he is called, is from Austria. He's jumped off some of the world's highest buildings, including the Petronas Towers in Malaysia and the Turning Torso in Sweden. In December 2007, he jumped from the 91st floor of Taipei 101 in Taiwan. When Felix jumps, he always uses a parachute. He hasn't had any bad accidents, but he's broken a few bones. He sprained his ankle when he jumped from Taipei 101.

He's been in trouble with the police a few times. The biggest problem is getting to the top of buildings with his parachute. He solved the problem in Sweden, when he jumped out of a helicopter and landed on the roof of the Turning Torso. So far Felix hasn't been in prison. Other BASE jumpers haven't been so lucky. When Jebb Corliss tried to jump off the Empire State Building in New York, the police arrested him and he lost his job as a TV reporter.

In his most recent adventures he hasn't jumped *off* things, but *into* things. He's done two jumps into caves—in Croatia and in Oman.

2 Check (✓) the things that he has done or that have happened to him.

☐ He's jumped off a bridge.   ☐ He lost his job as a TV reporter.   ☐ He's been in prison.

☐ He's jumped out of a helicopter.   ☐ He sprained his ankle in Taiwan.   ☐ He's jumped into a cave.

3 Write a short summary of the article.

Felix Baumgartner is from _____ . He's a _____ . He's jumped
                              1   2

off some of _____ including _____ and _____ .
                  3   4   5

In 2007, he jumped from the _____ in Taiwan.
                                   6

D EVERYDAY EXPRESSIONS: Reporting information

1 Number the parts of the story in the correct order.

_____ a. Ryan asks Lucy about her new job.

_____ b. They talk about Jordan and his new acting job, Sarah and her parents, Melanie and school, and Russell and his new apartment.

_1_ c. Ryan notices that Lucy doesn't look happy.

_____ d. Lucy tells Ryan about Rose, her new boss.

_____ e. Lucy tells Ryan that she's sad because her life isn't very exciting.

_____ f. Rose calls Lucy to say she'd like to talk to her.

2 Find the mistakes. Rewrite the expressions correctly.

1. I stand that Mira is coming home soon. _I understand that Mira is coming home soon._

2. Apparent Dora's boss hasn't been very nice to her. _____

3. It that seems my life isn't very exciting. _____

4. I feel that Jen met a guy. _____

3 Complete the conversation. Use the expressions from Activity 2. There are two choices for numbers 3 and 4.

A: Where's Francisco? He was supposed to be here by 10:00.

B: Oh, yes. I forgot to tell you. Francisco called. _____1_____ he's sick today.

A: Really? That is the fifth time this month. _____2_____ he's sick a lot!

B: I know what you mean. Actually, _____ / _____ that he's looking for another job.
3
Maybe he's out interviewing.

A: That's interesting. _____ / _____ that there are some job openings in Macon's
4
Department Store.

B: Maybe. He could be there right now.

4 Use the expressions to write your own conversation.

A: _____

B: _____

A: _____

B: _____

UNIT 6 Healthy living

A VOCABULARY: Health and fitness

1 Complete the expressions. Use the words in the box.

running	a swim	some stretching exercises	weight
a good night's sleep	~~salt~~	junk food	at the gym

1. cut down on _____salt_____   5. lose _____

2. do _____   6. give up _____

3. go _____   7. work out _____

4. get _____   8. go for _____

2 Write about two healthy things you have done this week and two things you haven't done.

1. I've _____been to the gym._____ .

2. I've _____ .

3. I haven't _____ .

4. I haven't _____ .

3 Complete the sentences. Write *for*, *to*, or – if nothing is needed.

1. Are you going _____ a walk?

2. We often go _____ cycling.

3. Do you ever go _____ the gym?

4. I go _____ an exercise class on Tuesdays.

5. We're going _____ swimming today.

6. I think I'll go _____ a run later today.

4 Complete the sentences about your lifestyle.

1. I _____ a lot of junk food.

2. I _____ the gym.

3. I _____ vitamins.

4. I _____ weight.

6. I _____ stretching exercises.

7. I _____ sleep.

8. I _____ diet.

B GRAMMAR: Future—*will/going to*

1 Circle the correct forms of the future tense.

Form	Use	Examples
will	general predictions	In the future we *won't / aren't going to* have cars.
	spontaneous plans	I don't have any money. I *'ll / 'm going to* go to the bank before going to the movies.
going to	things we are sure about	Oh, no. It's late. We *'ll / 're going to* miss the train.
	plans and decisions	We *'ll / 're going to* watch TV now.

2 Complete the responses with the verbs in parentheses. Then match the statements with the responses.

____ 1. Oh, no! I've spilled coffee on you.
____ 2. Oh, I forgot to buy a newspaper.
____ 3. I don't have time to reserve the tickets today.
____ 4. Would you like to go for a walk?

a. It's all right. I 'll do it online, later. (do)
b. OK. We ____________ one later. (buy)
c. Yes, I ____________ my coat. (get)
d. Don't worry. I ____________ change. (go)

3 Write two sentences about each picture.

1. 
2. 
3. 
4. 

1. Paolo 's going to relax. He isn't going to go for a walk. (relax / go for a walk)
2. We ____________ (go swimming / play tennis)
3. Lisa ____________ (lift weights / do yoga)
4. I ____________ (watch soccer / go to the gym)

4 Complete the sentences. Write the correct words from the parentheses.

1. **A:** Hal is going to call you at 3:00. (will / is going to)
   B: Oh, well, I'm going out, so I 'll call him now. ('ll / 'm going to)
2. **A:** ____________ play tennis on Saturday? (Will you / Are you going to)
   B: No, I can't. We ____________ look at a new apartment. ('ll / 're going to)
3. **A:** In the future we ____________ have any oil. (won't / aren't going to)
   B: Maybe, but we ____________ find new kinds of energy. ('ll / 're going to)
4. **A:** I've decided to change my lifestyle. From now on I ____________ eat a healthy diet. ('ll / 'm going to)
   B: Good idea. I ____________ join you. ('ll / 'm going to)

C READING AND WRITING: Healthy habits

1 Read the article. Then check (✓) the pictures that show healthy things to do, and put an X (X) next to the pictures that show unhealthy things to do.

Sleeping Tips

Sleep is very important. If you don't get a good night's sleep, you'll feel tired and stressed the next day. You won't enjoy life. If you find it difficult to get to sleep at night, here's some simple advice.

1. Always leave an hour to relax before you go to bed. When you work late at night, your brain stays busy. So, switch off the computer, sit comfortably, and watch TV or read a book. However, it's important that you don't fall asleep in your chair!

2. A lot of people like to have a cup of coffee after dinner, but the best advice is: don't! Think about it. We drink coffee in the morning to wake us up, so what is that espresso in the evening going to do? That's right. It's going to do exactly the same thing.

3. We all have busy lives, but rushing from one thing to another all day makes it hard to switch off at night. Find some time to relax during the day. Try this simple breathing exercise. Lie on the floor on your back. Put your arms by your side with your palms up. Close your eyes. Now, breathe in through your nose for four seconds. Hold it for six seconds, then slowly breathe out through your mouth for eight seconds. Repeat the exercise ten times. Doing this will make you more relaxed at bedtime.

Try these simple ideas and you will sleep well!

1. _____   3. _____   5. _____

2. _____   4. _____   6. _____

2 Check (✓) the parts of the body mentioned in the article.

_____ eyes   ✓ brain   _____ nose   _____ blood   _____ back   _____ arms

_____ mouth   _____ legs   _____ side   _____ palms   _____ stomach   _____ hand

4 Complete the sentences to write a short summary of the article.

"Sleeping Tips" is a good article for people who have trouble getting a _____. It gives

three pieces of _____. The first is about relaxing before you _____

instead of working late. The second is about not drinking coffee _____. The third

piece of advice is about relaxing _____, too. It suggests lying _____

and breathing slowly. It says to breathe in and out slowly _____.

D EVERYDAY EXPRESSIONS: Talking about relationships

1 Read the summary. <u>Underline</u> the seven mistakes.

Matt meets Sarah <u>in the park</u>. They talk about Sarah's visiting friends. Sarah is waiting for her father who is coming there to meet some of Sarah's teachers. Sarah forgets her wallet, so has to go back home. She asks Matt to wait there in case she's not back in time. Matt sees Sarah's mother. He tells her that Sarah is on her way back. Sarah's mother thinks Matt is Ryan. She explains that Sarah has told her everything about him. When Sarah returns, she brings Lucy with her to introduce to her mother. Sarah's mother is confused.

2 Rewrite the summary correctly.

Matt meets Sarah in the cafe. _____

_____

_____

_____

_____

_____

_____

3 Match the parts of the expressions.

_____ 1. They really enjoy   a. to know each other.

_____ 2. They have   b. a great relationship.

_____ 3. They can get   c. close.

_____ 4. They're very   d. each other's company.

4 Complete the conversation. Use the expressions in Activity 3.

A: Corinna's very excited because her parents are coming to meet her fiancé.

B: Yes, I heard that. That's great. Corinna and her parents have a _____ .
   They're _____ .
                      2

               1

A: Yes, that's what I heard. They really _____ .
                  3

B: Apparently they're going to spend a month here.

A: Great. Then her parents and her fiancé can _____ .
                  4

B: Yes, they can!

What a pain!

A VOCABULARY: Transportation problems

1 Complete the descriptions of the pictures. Use the words in the box.

| canceled | construction | accident | traffic | ~~broke down~~ | delayed |

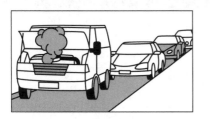

1. The road is blocked because a car _broke down_ .

2. They're stuck in _____ because of _____ .

3. All flights are _____ today.

4. The trains are _____. People will be late.

5. The bridge is closed because of an _____ .

2 Complete the sentences.

1. The police have closed the highway. The highway _____is closed_____ .

2. They've canceled our train. Our train _____ .

3. The weather is delaying all flights. All flights _____ .

4. Water has flooded the streets. The streets _____ .

3 Unscramble the words to complete the conversation.

A: Hello. I'm afraid we're going to be late. We were _____delayed_____ (eddyale) because the
                                                                        1

bridge was _____ (desolc). Now we're in terrible _____ (ficafrt) on the freeway.
                      2   3

B: Oh, no. Was there an _____ (dincacet)?
                                    4

A: No, I heard on the radio that a truck _____ (erkob wond) and now the road is blocked.
                                                    5

B: That's terrible.

A: Well, we wanted to come by train, but they were all _____ (elendacc) today!
                                                                          6

GRAMMAR: Past perfect

1 Complete the chart. Use the words in the box.

~~taken~~	hadn't	returned	'd

Past perfect: statements			
I	had	_taken_	the key.
He	_____		
They	had not	_____	it.
We	_____		

2 Complete the sentences. A check (✓) means to use the past perfect affirmative and an X (✗) means to use the past perfect negative.

1. We stayed at the Grand Hotel. We _____ hadn't stayed _____ there before. ✗

2. I broke my finger. I _____ the same one once before. ✓

3. We saw the Grand Canyon on vacation. We _____ it before. ✓

4. I did yoga yesterday. That was my first time. I _____ it before. ✗

5. She drove to Florida. She _____ there before. ✗

6. The bridge was closed. It _____ closed last week, too. ✓

3 Complete the conversations. Use the words in parentheses.

1. **A:** The roads were flooded.

   B: _____ Had there been _____ a lot of rain? (there / be)

   A: Yes, _____.

2. **A:** She won the cycling race.

   B: _____ it before? (she / win)

   A: No, _____.

3. **A:** We took the train to Chicago.

   B: _____ it before? (you / take)

   A: No, _____.

4. **A:** Someone returned my briefcase.

   B: _____ it on the train again? (you / leave)

   A: Yes, _____.

4 Complete the sentences.

1. The car broke down. We arrived late.

   We arrived late because _____ the car had broken down _____.

2. I forgot her name. I felt embarrassed.

   I felt embarrassed because _____.

3. I didn't take a key. I locked myself out.

   I locked myself out because _____.

1 Read the conversation. What was in each suitcase?

> **Adam:** Something very strange happened to me earlier this year. I'd been away on business for about ten days in Houston. I'd taken the train because I don't like flying. When I got home, I couldn't open my suitcase.
>
> **Isabel:** Oh, no! Had you taken someone else's?
>
> **Adam:** Yes! When I looked at it closely, I could see that it wasn't mine.
>
> **Isabel:** Do you think somebody had the same kind of suitcase and took yours by mistake?
>
> **Adam:** Yes, I think so! So, I took it to the police station and they opened it. And... then they arrested me.
>
> **Isabel:** Why? Because you'd taken someone's suitcase by mistake?
>
> **Adam:** Well, no. Because the suitcase was full of stolen money and jewelry.
>
> **Isabel:** Wow! But jewelry and money are heavy. Hadn't you noticed?
>
> **Adam:** No, because I'd brought a lot of heavy reports back from my business trip.
>
> **Isabel:** Oh, right. So what happened?
>
> **Adam:** I spent hours at the police station. They asked me lots of questions, but in the end they believed me.
>
> **Isabel:** And did they find the person that the suitcase belonged to?
>
> **Adam:** I don't know, but I bet they got a big surprise when they opened my suitcase. It was full of dirty clothes and a lot of boring reports!

2 Answer the questions.

1. Where had Adam been?

2. How long had he been there?

3. Why couldn't Adam open the suitcase?

4. Why did the police arrest him?

5. What happened at the police station?

3 Circle the correct sentence connectors.

_____*Because / When*_____ Adam went to Houston earlier this year, he took the train
                1

_____*because / and*_____ he doesn't like flying. _____*When / But*_____ he got home, he tried to open his
           2   3

suitcase, ____*so / but*____ he couldn't. He looked at it closely _____*but / and*_____ saw that it wasn't his,
              4   5

_____*so / because*_____ he took it to the police station _____*when / and*_____ the police opened it.
           6   7

D EVERYDAY EXPRESSIONS: Showing sympathy

1 Choose the correct words to complete the summary.

Jordan is talking to ___*Peter / Matt*___ at
                              1
Cozy Cup. He has a ___*headache / cold*___ . It
                              2
started ___*over the weekend / on Monday*___ . He didn't
                              3
go to visit Lucy's ___*grandparents / parents*___ .
                              4
Lucy was very ___*happy / annoyed*___ when Jordan
                              5
told her, because she ___*was / wasn't*___ really
                              6
looking forward to it. Jordan didn't go because he got a part in ___*a play / a TV show*___ . He was a
                              7
___*jogger / dog walker*___ in a park. However, the weekend went really ___*badly / well*___ . It
         8   9
___*snowed / rained*___ all day on Saturday, so they couldn't do anything. It ___*rained / didn't rain*___
         10   11
on Sunday, but there was a very ___*cold / warm*___ wind. Jordan was only wearing
                              12
___*jeans / shorts*___ and a T-shirt, so he was ___*freezing / hot*___ . He thinks that's how
         13   14
he ___*got / found*___ his cold. And it was a complete waste of ___*money / time*___ anyway.
         15   16
They ___*cut / didn't cut*___ his scene because it was ___*not long enough / too long*___ .
         17   18

2 Circle the five sympathy expressions in the word snake.

icanimaginepooryouthat'sashameblessyouthatstoobad

3 Complete the conversation. Use the expressions from Activity 3.

A: I don't feel well.

B: ___*Poor you*___ . Do you have a cold?
              1

A: No, I think I have the flu.

B: Oh, no.

A: I just want to go to home and go to bed.

B: Yes, I _____ .
                 2

A: I have a ticket for a show tonight, too, but I don't want to go now.

B: _____ bad. I'm afraid I'm busy this evening, so I can't use it.
         3

A: That's _____ . *Achoo!*
                 4

B: _____ ! I think you should go to bed.
         5

8 Eat up!

A VOCABULARY: Describing food

1 Write the words that describe each food.

sour	rare	spicy	sweet	salty	strong

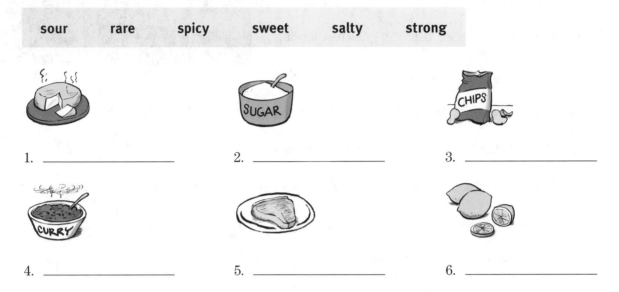

1. _____

2. _____

3. _____

4. _____

5. _____

6. _____

2 Write the pairs of opposites.

crispy	raw	dry	soft	~~sweet~~	juicy	cooked	~~sour~~

1. _____sweet_____ _____sour_____   3. _____ _____

2. _____ _____   4. _____ _____

3 Put the descriptions of meat in the correct order.

well-done	rare	medium	raw

1. _____

2. _____

3. _____

4. _____well-done_____

4 Complete the descriptions.

1. This sauce has a lot of cream in it. The sauce is very _____creamy_____.

2. Fish that has a lot of oil is good for you. _____ fish is good for you.

3. Does this soup have a lot of spices in it? Is this soup _____?

4. That steak has a lot of fat on it. That steak is very _____.

GRAMMAR: Tag questions

1 Complete the rules with *affirmative* or *negative*.

Tag questions		
_____affirmative_____ verb +	_____	tag
_____ verb +	_____	tag

2 Use the words in the box to complete the tags. There are two extras.

don't	can	isn't	can't	do

1. You don't drink tea, _____ you?

2. She can join us, _____ she?

3. Carlos is from Spain, _____ he?

3 Complete the sentences. Write the correct form of the verbs.

1. You can swim, _____can't_____ you? (*can / can't*)

2. The food was very salty, _____ it? (*was / wasn't*)

3. You don't like rare steak, _____ you? (*do / don't*)

4. They don't have any children, _____ they? (*do / don't*)

5. This is your car, _____ it? (*is / isn't*)

6. The store won't be open tomorrow, _____ it? (*will / won't*)

4 Complete the tag questions. Use the correct tense.

1. You're an engineer, _____aren't you_____?

2. It's going to be hot today, _____?

3. Your wife can sing, _____?

4. Pierre isn't coming with us, _____?

5. You didn't like the movie, _____?

6. Maria doesn't work here now, _____?

7. They won't be here Monday, _____?

8. You have the car keys, _____?

5 Complete the tag questions. Then answer the questions about you.

1. You aren't married, _____are you_____?   _Yes, I am. / No, I'm not._

2. You're a student, _____?   _____

3. You haven't been to Canada, _____?   _____

4. You can cook, _____?   _____

5. You live downtown, _____?   _____

6. You went to a restaurant yesterday, _____?   _____

C READING AND WRITING: Ordering Chinese food

1 Read the conversation between Yao Mei and Antonia. Then check (✓) the foods they order.

☐ chicken chow mein ☐ Sichuan orange beef ☐ shrimp crackers ☐ boiled rice

☐ sweet and sour pork ☐ spicy hotpot ☐ fried rice ☐ bread

Yao Mei: This is a great restaurant. The prices are really reasonable. It's a Sichuan restaurant. You've had Sichuan food before, haven't you, Antonia?

Antonia: Well, I've been to lots of Chinese restaurants before. It's just Chinese food, isn't it?

Yao Mei: Yes, but there are lots of different kinds of Chinese food. Sichuan is in the southern part of China, and the food there is hot and spicy.

Antonia: Oh, I see. Well, I like spicy food. So, what's on the menu?

Yao Mei: Well, they have chicken chow mein. That's chicken cooked with noodles.

Antonia: I've had that before. I liked it, but I'd prefer trying something new.

Yao Mei: OK. Well, there's sweet and sour pork. Actually that's very good here. It's fried pork marinated in a sauce made with pineapples and lime juice.

Antonia: I'm afraid I don't really like pineapples. What else do you recommend?

Yao Mei: Sichuan orange beef. It's beef fried with honey and orange juice. It's really delicious.

Antonia: Yes, it sounds delicious. What's this? The spicy hotpot?

Yao Mei: It's a kind of soup. It's made with vegetables – cabbage, mushrooms, onions, and chilies. It's served in a big pot in the middle of the table.

Antonia: Oh, so do you share it?

Yao Mei: Yes, but you actually use it to cook your food. You get pieces of meat, fish, shrimp, and some vegetables. They're all raw and you cook them in the hot soup.

Antonia: Well, that sounds like fun, doesn't it? Let's have that with fried rice.

2 Mark the statements true (T) or false (F).

_____ 1. Sichuan is part of China.

_____ 2. Sichuan food is not spicy.

_____ 3. Antonia has never eaten Chinese food.

_____ 4. Antonia doesn't like pineapples.

_____ 5. Yao Mei doesn't eat beef.

_____ 6. The spicy hotpot is only for one person.

3 Complete this description of the spicy hotpot.

With the _____(1)_____ hotpot you get pieces of _____(2)_____ fish,

_____(3)_____, shrimp, and some vegetables. You _____(4)_____ them at

your table in a _____(5)_____ of _____(6)_____. The soup is made with

_____(7)_____, such as cabbage, _____(8)_____, onions, and chilies.

D EVERYDAY EXPRESSIONS: Making complaints

1 Match the parts of the complaints.

_____ 1. This is not what I   a. not well-done.

_____ 2. This hamburger is   b. complain to the manager.

_____ 3. I'd like to   c. ordered.

2 Complete Mr. Tyler's letter of complaint to the manager.
Use the words in the box.

disappointing	table	group	complain	arrived
apologized	reserved	sincerely	available	hostess
record	~~Ms. Fowler~~	service		

Dear _____Ms. Fowler_____,
          1

    I am writing to _____ about the very poor _____
                    2   3

I received at your restaurant this evening. I had _____ a
                                                         4

_____ for a large _____ of people yesterday. However,
    5   6

when we _____, the _____ told me that there was no
           7   8

_____ of my reservation in the computer. The hostess
    9

_____, but she told me that there was nothing _____
    10   11

until 9:30. It was very _____, especially as it was my friend's birthday.
                      12

I look forward to hearing from you about this. _____,
                                                   13
G. Tyler

3 Think of an experience you would like to complain about. Write a complaint note.

Dear _____,

    I am writing to complain about _____

_____

_____

_____

_____

GET CONNECTED

Understanding the benefits of gaming

There are many advantages to online gaming. Different types of games have different kinds of benefits.

>> **Logic games** like *Sudoku* require focus, concentration, and problem-solving. They are a good source of mental exercise, and they can help players develop memory skills, language skills, and math skills.

>> **Speed games** like *Bejeweled* require players to look at many different moving objects on a screen and hit the objects or move them around. They may help improve players' hand-eye coordination and reaction time.

>> **Role-playing, multi-player games** like *Second Life* can help reduce stress because of the social interaction involved. They can also help players improve problem-solving skills, social skills, and teamwork skills.

GET Started

GET Together

1. Look at the online games on page 37. Write the name of each game next to the correct type of game below.

1. logic game _____

2. speed game _____

3. role-playing, multi-player game _____

2. Work with a partner. Discuss the questions below and write your answers.

1. Which type of game do you think is the most fun? Why?

_____

_____

2. Which type of game do you think has the most advantages or benefits? Why?

_____

_____

3. What are some possible disadvantages of each type of game?

_____

_____

> > > >

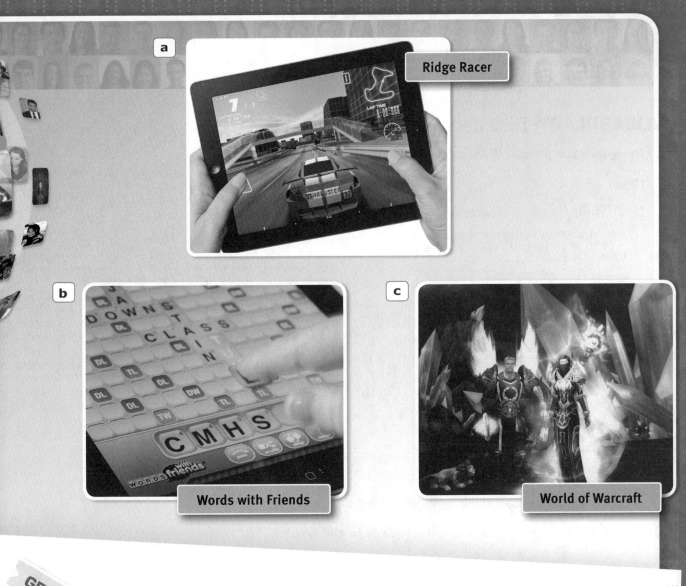

a Ridge Racer

b Words with Friends

c World of Warcraft

3 Think of or find one online game for each category. How do you play each game?
What are important benefits of each game? Complete the chart below.

Type of game	Name of game	How you play	Benefits of this game
Logic			
Speed			
Role-playing multi-player			

> > > > > **Now I can...** understand the benefits of online gaming.

☐ Not at all ☐ Well ☐ Very well

Take it online
Play one logic game and one speed game.

37

What a disaster!

A VOCABULARY: Disasters

1 Complete the puzzle. What is the hidden word in gray?

Clues

1. The water in the rivers rose and rose until they spilled over and caused a _____ .

2. _____ and tropical storms are named in alphabetical order.

3. A 7.2 _____ on the coast caused many buildings to fall down.

4. A _____ has broken out in the San Gabriel mountains.

5. The lack of rain caused a terrible _____ .

6. The wave grew bigger and bigger until it became a _____ .

2 Complete the news reports. Use the words in the box.

there has been	was the result of	has damaged	has caused
break out	there are (x2)	have destroyed	has hit (x 2)

1. A hurricane _____ has hit _____ the coast of Florida. The high winds _____ many buildings.

2. _____ no rain in parts of central Africa for a very long time. This _____ one of their worst droughts in many years.

3. The strong winds and dry air have caused several forest fires to _____ in the mountains. _____ thousands of firefighters from all over the state fighting the fires.

4. A tsunami _____ an island in the Pacific Ocean. The wave _____ an earthquake near the east coast of Australia.

5. After a week of heavy rain, _____ floods in many parts of central Europe. The water _____ thousands of buildings.

B GRAMMAR: First and second conditionals

1 Circle the correct verbs.

1. I *was / would be* worried about earthquakes if I *lived / would live* in California.

2. If an earthquake *happened / would happen*, what *did / would* you do?

3. If I *were / would be* indoors, I *didn't / wouldn't* run outside.

4. If there *was / would be* a table in the room, I *got / would* get under it.

5. I *stood / would stand* in a doorway if there *wasn't / wouldn't be* a table there.

6. If I *were / would be* outside, I *moved / would move* away from the buildings.

2 Complete the chart. Choose the correct form of the verbs to complete the example sentences.

past	imaginary	present
will (x2)	possible	would (x2)

	First conditional	**Second conditional**
Use	likely or _____ events	unlikely or _____ events
Tenses: *if* clause	_____ simple	_____ simple
Main clause	_____ future	_____ conditional
Examples	If I get up late tomorrow, my boss _____ be angry.	If I got up late every day, I _____ lose my job.

3 Complete the sentences. Write the correct form of the verbs in parentheses. Then check (✓) the imaginary situation.

1. a. If it _____ again tomorrow, we won't go out. (*rains / rained*)

   b. If it rained like this every day, the river _____ the town. (*will flood / would flood*)

2. a. If we fly to Canada, it _____ three hours. (*will take / would take*)

   b. We _____ the train if we had more time. (*will take / would take*)

3. a. We wouldn't have global warming if people _____ less energy. (*use / used*)

   b. If gas prices _____ again, I'll sell my car. (*go up / went up*)

4 Complete the sentences about your own life.

1. If I were younger, _____ I'd travel more. _____ .

2. If I go to bed late tonight, _____ .

3. If there were eight days in a week, I _____ on my extra day.

4. If the weather's nice this weekend, _____ .

C READING AND WRITING: A tough job

1 Read the article. Complete the summary below.

Search and Rescue

If you heard that the weather was terrible, what would you do? Most people would stay indoors and watch TV. But not Jim Fletcher. Even if he's in bed and the phone rings, he'll get dressed, put on his boots, collect his equipment, and drive into the hills.

Jim is a member of the Mountain Rescue Service. There are lots of lakes, hills, and mountains in the area, so it's a popular destination for walkers and climbers. If someone has an accident or gets lost, Jim and the other members of the team will go and rescue them—24 hours a day, 365 days a year.

There are usually 16 people in a team. Their first job is to find the people who are in trouble. If someone is injured, the team will carry the person down. Sometimes they can't move the person. If that happens, they'll call for a helicopter.

Everyone in the team is an experienced climber and there's always a doctor, too. Unfortunately, accidents sometimes happen when the weather is bad and the team has to go out at night. As Jim explains, "People will often call the Mountain Rescue Service if someone doesn't come home at the end of the day. It's usually dark by then, especially in winter, when the days are short."

"We wouldn't have so many accidents," says Jim, "if people were more careful. A lot of visitors don't understand that the hills can be dangerous. The weather here can change very quickly. Things like thunderstorms, high winds, heavy rain, and fog are common."

lost	rescue	team	hills	accident	members

With other _____ of his _____ , Jim helps to _____ people who have
          1   2   3

had an _____ or gotten _____ in the _____ .
       4   5   6

2 Complete Jim's answers to the questions.

1. **A:** Do you go out every day of the year?

   Jim: _____ .

2. **A:** How many people are there in a team?

   Jim: _____ .

3. **A:** How do you bring people down from the hills usually?

   Jim: _____ .

4. **A:** What will you do if you can't move the person?

   Jim: _____ .

D EVERYDAY EXPRESSIONS: Talking about telephoning

1 Match the two parts of the sentences.

_____ 1. Everyone is sorry

_____ 2. Yuka has talked to her sister, but

_____ 3. Ryan suggests that maybe the phone

_____ 4. Yuka's parents' phone

_____ 5. Yuka's going to try

_____ 6. Yuka reaches her parents and learns

_____ 7. Yuka decides to

a. service is out.

b. to call some other numbers.

c. go home to help her parents.

d. rings, but there's no answer.

e. she hasn't been able to reach her parents.

f. that the tsunami flooded their store.

g. to hear about the earthquake in Japan.

2 Circle the correct words to complete the expressions.

1. **A:** I'm calling Morgan. It's _ringing / rings_, but there's no answer.

   B: Maybe they're all in a meeting.

   A: At last! Hello. Can I... ? No, don't hang _off / up_! I don't believe it!

2. **A:** _There's / It's_ no answer at Frank's office, so I'll _try / reply_ his cell phone.

   B: If it's very important, you can call his wife. Do you have her _number / phone_?

   A: No. Good idea. She will be able to _reach / grab_ him.

3 Complete the conversation. Use the expressions in Activity 2.

A: Who are you calling?

B: Tess, but there's no _____ .
                                1

A: Have you tried her cell phone?

B: Yes. I've tried her landline and her cell phone. I just can't _____ her.
                                                                       2

A: Is there another _____ you can try? How about her boyfriend's cell phone?
                          3

B: I'll just try one more time.

A: Oh, what's that sound? I think I hear her phone _____ in the other room.
                                                        4
I guess she left it here!

A VOCABULARY: Computer words

1 Label this picture.

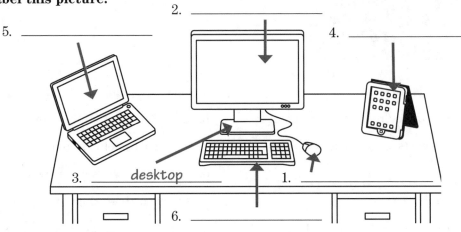

5. _____
2. _____
4. _____
3. _desktop_
1. _____
6. _____

2 Complete the questionnaire. Check the boxes that apply, circle *yes* or *no*, and use the words in the box.

games	DVDs	laptop	Internet	what
modem	school	cafe	use	screen
e-mail	mouse	social	tablet	listening to

1. Where do you _____ a computer?
   - [ ] at work / _____
   - [ ] at home

2. Do you ever go to an Internet _____ ? yes / no

3. Which do you use more often?
   - [ ] a desktop
   - [ ] a _____
   - [ ] a _____

4. When you use a laptop, do you ever connect a _____ to it? yes / no

5. When you use a laptop, do you ever connect it to a _____ for your Internet connection? yes / no

6. When you work on a laptop, does the size of the _____ matter to you? yes / no

7. _____ do you use a computer for the most? Rank these from 1 to 9, with 1 being the activity you do the most.
   - [ ] word processing
   - [ ] checking your _____
   - [ ] playing _____
   - [ ] surfing the Internet
   - [ ] reading news
   - [ ] _____ music
   - [ ] shopping or purchasing tickets
   - [ ] watching TV or _____
   - [ ] _____ networking

8. How much time do you spend on the _____ each day? Circle one:

   Less than one hour

   between one and two hours

   between two and three hours

   more than three hours

B GRAMMAR: *used to/didn't use to*

1 Complete the chart with *use* and *used* and choose the correct ending for the rule.

used to	
Affirmative	**Negative**
I _____ to work in a store.	I didn't _____ to work in an office.
We use *used to* for states and events that were true in the past, *and are still true / but aren't true now*.	

2 Complete the sentences. Use *used to* and the verbs in parentheses.

1. He _____ used to work _____ on a laptop. (work)

2. I _____ to Internet cafes. (go)

3. They _____ basketball on Wednesdays. (play)

4. She _____ a bicycle to work. (ride)

3 Make the sentences in Activity 2 negative.

1. He ____ didn't use to work on a laptop ____.

2. I _____.

3. They _____.

4. She _____.

4 Write the sentences. Use *used to* or *didn't use to* and the words in the box.

work here	~~live in San Diego~~	eat meat
wear glasses	be married	be so thin

1. She doesn't live in San Diego now. ____ She used to live in San Diego. ____

2. He's lost a lot of weight. _____

3. I wear glasses now. _____

4. They got divorced last year. _____

5. I was a vegetarian for a long time. _____

6. She joined the company last week. _____

5 Answer the questions about when you were a child.

1. Who used to be your best friend? _____.

2. What school did you use to go to? _____.

3. Did you use to have a pet? _____.

4. Where did you use to go on vacation? _____.

C READING AND WRITING: A story in the past

1 **Read the story. Match the names with the descriptions and the countries.**

The best time of my life

My name's Eva and I'm from Poland. When I was in college, I used to be a tour guide. One day, one of the American tourists in my group was a scientist. His name was John Reed. He was studying the birds of the rainforest in Costa Rica. He asked if I would like to join his research team. As soon as I finished college, I set off to Costa Rica.

We stayed at a research station near the coast. We slept in small huts—two people in one hut. There were showers, but only cold water! We got up very early in the morning, at about 5:00 a.m., and after breakfast we drove into the forest. It was hard work because we had to carry all of our equipment with us.

In the forest we caught birds. Then we photographed, measured, and weighed them. My main job as an assistant was to put all the information into a laptop. It was very hot in the forest, and there were lots of tropical insects. I used to be afraid of them, but after a while, I stopped being so afraid.

It wasn't all work, however. We didn't use to work on the weekends. We either relaxed or visited other parts of the country. We were near the coast, so we spent a lot of time on the beach swimming, sunbathing, and playing volleyball. In the evening, we ate together, and after dinner we used to sing or tell stories. The food was good. Victor, the chef at the research station, used to cook wonderful local dishes.

I learned a lot during my time in Costa Rica, and I met some very interesting people. After six months, however, I decided to give it up. It was time for me to go home and look for a full-time job. I look back on those six months as the best time of my life!

_b, h_ Eva	a. the chef	e. the U.S.
_____ John Reed	b. a tour guide and student	f. Costa Rica
_____ Giulia	c. a scientist	g. Italy
_____ Victor	d. Eva's roommate	h. Poland

2 **Mark the statements true (T) or false (F).**

_T_   1. Eva was a student in Poland.

_____   2. She had her own room at the research station.

_____   3. She used to take a hot shower every day.

_____   4. The team used to get up at 5:00 in the morning.

_____   5. They used to go into the forest by boat.

_____   6. Eva's main job was to weigh and measure the birds.

_____   7. She has always liked spiders.

_____   8. The members of the team didn't work on Saturdays.

D EVERYDAY EXPRESSIONS: Talking about changes

1 Complete the summary. Use the words in the box.

finished	work	remember	~~talking~~
recognize	talk	part	actor
happened	changed	enjoy	got

Peter and Lucy are _____talking_____ about Melanie. She was at
                              1

college, but she's _____ now. Peter doesn't
                        2

_____ her because she's _____
        3   4

a lot. Lucy says she can _____ when Melanie was
                                  5

in high school and she used to _____ in the cafe on
                                        6

the weekends. Melanie comes over to _____ to
                                              7

Peter and Lucy. Melanie asks Peter what's _____ to Jordan. She says that she used
                                                  8

to _____ talking to him. Peter explains that Jordan is an _____
        9   10

and that he _____ a _____ in a soap opera.
                    11   12

2 Put the words in the correct order to complete the expressions.

1. Melanie _____has changed a lot_____. (changed / a / has / lot)

2. That seems like _____. (long / a / ago / time)

3. Whatever _____ who used to work here? (happened / girl / that / to)

4. What _____? (up / 's / to / days / these / she)

5. _____? (fly / time / doesn't)

6. _____ she used to sing here. (when / I / remember / can)

3 Complete the conversation. Use the sentences in Activity 2.

A: Whatever _____happened to that girl_____ who used to work here—the one from Brazil?
                          1

B: Celina? I _____ she used to sing here. At the karaoke nights.
                      2

A: Oh yes. She was great! That seems like _____.
                                                    3

B: Yes, we used to have a lot of fun back then.

A: That's true. It's much quieter now. This place _____.
                                                            4

B: _____?
            5

A: Yes. Anyway, what about Celina? What _____?
                                                    6

B: I have no idea. I haven't seen her since she left.

Crime and punishment

A VOCABULARY: Criminal activities

1 **Match the words with their meanings.**

_____ 1. a criminal   a. a place where criminals are sent

_____ 2. robbing   b. person who commits a crime

_____ 3. a witness   c. stealing things

_____ 4. a crime   d. a person who sees a crime

_____ 5. a victim   e. a person that a crime is committed against

_____ 6. prison   f. murder or blackmail, etc.

2 **Complete the text. Use the words in the box.**

committed	stole	victims	robberies	prison
crimes	arrested	criminals	witnesses	~~robbers~~

Two ___robbers___ will go to _____ for five years. The police
        1   2

_____ them after they _____ bags, purses, and wallets. The
   3   4

_____ were tourists in a popular beach town. The _____ are a man
   5   6

and woman, both 23 years old. Fortunately, three _____ saw the _____
                                     7   8

from a nearby window. The robbers have _____ several _____ before.
                                         9   10

3 **Complete each sentence with _robbed_ and _stole_.**

1. Three people ___stole___ $10 million when they ___robbed___ a bank in Boston.

2. A man _____ a supermarket and _____ some money.

3. Thieves _____ passports when they _____ a group of tourists.

4. Two men _____ a jewelry store. They _____ some diamonds and watches.

5. Thieves _____ the art gallery last night and _____ several paintings.

4 **Complete the chart. Use the words in the box.**

~~a bank~~   money   a supermarket   jewelry   an art gallery   diamonds

Robbers rob	___a bank___, _____, _____
Robbers steal	_____, _____, _____

B GRAMMAR: Narrative tenses

1 Write the name of the tense with the correct example.

past continuous	past simple	past perfect

When John looked around, someone...	
Tense	**Example**
	stole his cell phone.
	was stealing his cell phone.
	had stolen his cell phone.

2 Complete the story. Use the verbs in parentheses in the past perfect.

Chloe came out of the restaurant and went to her car. She ___*had parked*___ (park) it in a

              1

street near the restaurant. She _____ (not park) in the restaurant parking lot,

              2

because it _____ (be) full. When she got to her car, the alarm was sounding and the

           3

lights were flashing. Someone _____ (try) to steal it while she _____

              4   5

(be) in the restaurant.

3 Complete the sentences. Use the verbs in parentheses in the past continuous.

Chloe called the police. When they arrived, ...

1. the car alarm ___*wasn't sounding*___. (not sound)

2. the lights _____. (not flash)

3. Chloe _____ her cell phone. (use)

4. she _____ pictures of the damage. (take)

5. some people _____ out of their windows. (look)

4 Circle the correct verb forms.

Eric was at the station. He *waited / was waiting* for his train home. He *had put / was putting*

                                            1   2

his briefcase on the ground and he *read / was reading* a newspaper. While he

                                          3

had stood / was standing there, his phone was ___*ringing / rang*___. It was his wife. While

          4   5

Eric ___*talk / was talking*___ to her, the train ___*arrived / was arriving*___. Eric

             6   7

was bending down / bent down to pick up his briefcase, but it was gone. Someone

         8

stole / had stolen it while he *wasn't looking / didn't look*.

         9   10

C READING AND WRITING: A crime story

1 Read the article. Match the people to the descriptions.

The Oxford Detective

One evening in September, two young women were hitchhiking near the English city of Oxford. A few hours later, one of them was dead. Sylvia Kaye's body was found in a parking lot. The police found her purse, but it was empty except for an envelope with a piece of paper inside. On the paper were three words: "Take this, please." Who had killed Sylvia Kaye? What had happened to her friend? Who had written the strange message?

It was the first case for Inspector Morse—one of the most popular fictional detectives. *Last Bus to Woodstock* was Colin Dexter's first novel about the quiet but brilliant detective. Morse went on to appear in twelve more novels and several short stories. With his young assistant, Sergeant Lewis, he drove around the city of Oxford in his old Jaguar, dealing with numerous cases of murder, robbery, blackmail, and suicide.

In 1987, the books became a TV series with the actor John Thaw as Morse. People in Oxford often saw them when they were filming in the city. The series became an international success.

Morse finally died in the novel, *The Remorseful Day*. He had a heart attack as he was walking through the streets of Oxford. As his creator, Colin Dexter, said, "Morse hadn't had a very healthy lifestyle. He'd worked long hours, and hadn't slept enough." Even so, it was a sad day for millions of TV viewers.

___c___ 1. Inspector Morse   a. the actor who played Morse

_____ 2. Colin Dexter   b. a murder victim in the first novel

_____ 3. Sergeant Lewis   c. a fictional detective

_____ 4. Sylvia Kaye   d. Morse's assistant

_____ 5. John Thaw   e. the author of the Morse books

2 Complete the sentences about Morse.

1. He worked in _____Oxford_____ .

2. He drove a _____ .

3. He didn't have a _____ lifestyle.

4. He _____ too many hours.

5. He hadn't _____ enough.

6. He died of a _____ .

3 Answer the questions.

1. What was the first Morse novel called? _____ .

2. When did the TV series start? _____ .

3. How many Morse novels did Colin Dexter write? _____ .

4. What was the last novel called? _____ .

5. What famous fictional detectives do you know? _____ .

D EVERYDAY EXPRESSIONS: Expressions with *when*

1 **Number the parts of the story in the correct order.**

_____ a. Matt suggests that Jordan uploads some video clips of his acting so that he can share them on a website.

_____ b. Jordan says that Lucy is mad at him because he has missed so many things. Matt suggests that Jordan surprise Lucy with tickets to see a great band.

_____ c. Lucy sees Jordan in line at the club. She gets very angry because Jordan told her he was working.

_____ d. Matt asks Jordan how Lucy is doing because he hasn't seen her in a while.

_____ e. Jordan tells Lucy that he was buying tickets as a surprise so that they could go together.

__1__ f. Matt asks to borrow Jordan's tablet because somebody stole his laptop.

_____ g. Jordan tells Matt that he played the part of a dying patient on a soap opera. As a result, his role didn't last long.

2 **Complete the conversation. Use the expressions from Activity 3.**

A: I took the car this morning, honey. You weren't awake yet, so I couldn't tell you.

B: I can't _____ you do that. I was an hour late for work!
           ₁

A: I _____ you take the car usually. I just really didn't want to wait for the
         ₂
bus this morning.

B: Please don't do that again. It _____ you don't listen to me. I can't be late
                                        ₃
for work anymore, my boss isn't happy about it.

A: How about if we buy a new car? Then we can both drive to work every day.

B: I _____ you make suggestions like that. What a great idea!
         ₄

A: Now I just have to figure out how to pay for it.

3 **Answer the questions about yourself.**

1. It bothers me when _____.

2. I like it when _____.

3. I don't mind it when _____.

4. I can't stand it when _____.

A VOCABULARY: Describing a festival

1 **Match the two parts of the sentences to describe the American holiday Halloween.**

_____ 1. People celebrate this holiday   a. giving candy to children.

_____ 2. This holiday has many traditions, such as   b. costumes.

_____ 3. People decorate their houses with   c. the pumpkin.

_____ 4. A common symbol of that holiday is   d. on October 31.

_____ 5. Children wear different kinds of   e. scary things like skeletons and ghosts.

2 **Complete the text. Use the words in the box.**

celebrate	special	remember	costumes
tradition	decorate	symbols	~~holiday~~

In the U.S., Thanksgiving is a _____holiday_____ Americans _____ on the
                                                       1   2

fourth Thursday of November. It is called Thanksgiving because it is a day of giving thanks. People

like to _____ all the good things in their lives. Many people have the
                    3

_____ of telling each other what they are thankful for during the Thanksgiving meal.
     4

The food is very _____ at Thanksgiving. People eat turkey and fruits and vegetables.
          5

The turkey is one of the _____ of Thanksgiving, and some people _____
          6   7

their dining tables with a colorful paper turkey. Many schools have Thanksgiving plays in which

the children dress up in Native American and Pilgrim _____.
                                                        8

3 **Answer the questions about a holiday or festival that you celebrate.**

1. What is the name of the holiday or festival? _____.

2. When is it? _____.

3. What do people do on that day? _____.

4. What is one tradition of that holiday or festival? _____.

5. How do people decorate for it? _____.

6. What is a common symbol of that holiday or festival? _____.

B GRAMMAR: Passives

1 Complete the chart.

Present simple passive			
Subject	**form of *to be***	**Past participle**	
This holiday	_____	celebrated	every year.
Those holidays	are	celebrated	
Past simple passive			
The house	was	decorated	beautifully last year.
The children	_____	dressed	

2 Complete the sentences. Use *is* or *are* and the past participle of the verb in parentheses.

1. The guests _____ *are invited* _____ to arrive around 2:00. (invite)

2. Holiday recipes _____ in special cookbooks. (find)

3. Shopping lists _____ the week before. (write)

4. The shopping _____ the day before. (do)

5. The house _____ today. (clean)

6. Decorations _____ around the house. (put up)

7. The table _____ for twelve people. (set)

8. The guests _____ to eat around 3:30. (welcome)

3 Change the sentences in Activity 2 to the past simple passive.

1. _____ *The guests were invited to arrive around 2:00.* _____

2. _____

3. _____

4. _____

5. _____

6. _____

7. _____

8. _____

4 Write sentences about a holiday or festival that you celebrated recently. Use the past simple passive.

1. _____

2. _____

3. _____

4. _____

C READING AND WRITING: A very old festival

1 **Read the article. What time of year is this festival?**

Nowruz

Nowruz is one of the oldest festivals in the world. It is celebrated in various countries in the Middle East and Asia, such as Iran, Afghanistan, and parts of northwestern China. The festival was first celebrated nearly 4,000 years ago. Nowruz is celebrated on the first day of spring to welcome the New Year. It lasts for thirteen days. For people who celebrate Nowruz, it is one of the most important festivals of the year.

Preparation for Nowruz begins very early in March. The houses are thoroughly cleaned, and new clothes are purchased for everyone in the family. Desserts are baked, and special foods are prepared. Singers parade through the streets singing about the beginning of the New Year. In every home a special table is prepared. The festival table is called the haft sin (haft = seven, sin = the letter s). Seven things are put on the table to celebrate Nowruz. The name of each thing must begin with the letter s, such as seeb – an apple. People put flowers, fruit, coins, candles, mirrors, and even goldfish on their table.

On the first day of Nowruz fires are lit, and people jump over them to bring good luck. There's a lot of eating and dancing during Nowruz. On the last day of the festival, it's bad luck to stay inside your house, so everyone eats outside.

Nowruz is celebrated in about 15 countries. In 2010, it was formally recognized by the United Nations. Nowruz was also officially registered on a Cultural Heritage UNESCO list.

2 **Read the text. Circle the correct words.**

1. The name of the festival is *Nowruz / Haft Sin*.

2. It's celebrated mainly in the Middle East and *Asia / Australia*.

3. The festival is to *say thank you for fire / welcome the New Year*.

4. The festival table has *seven / thirteen* things on it.

5. On the thirteenth day of Nowruz, it's *good / bad* luck to have a picnic outside.

3 **Answer the questions.**

1. How old is the festival?
   _____

2. When is it celebrated?
   _____

3. How long does it last?
   _____

4. What do people jump over?
   _____

5. What is the haft sin?
   _____

6. How many things are put on the table?
   _____

4 **Find these things in the article.**

1. Two countries where the festival is celebrated: _____

2. Six things that people put on the haft sin table: _____

D EVERYDAY EXPRESSIONS: Responding to information

1 Circle the correct words to complete the summary.

Sarah's parents ___*tell / are told*___ Sarah they
         1

want to spend more time with Peter. They want to

___*get him / get to know him*___ better. They ask
         2

Sarah to invite Peter to their friends' Halloween

party. Other friends of Sarah's parents

___*will invite / are invited*___, too, so it will be
         3

a good time for everyone to ___*meet / introduce to*___ Peter. Sarah invites Peter to the party and
                4

she tells him to get "dressed up." He asks Ryan what ___*is meant / means*___ by "dressed up." Ryan
                5

doesn't ___*thinking / realize*___ that it is a Halloween party. He thinks "dressed up" means wearing a
      6

suit. Ryan ___*advises / gives advice*___ Peter to wear a suit. Peter ___*has / wants to*___ make a
        7   8

good impression. When Peter arrives, everyone ___*surprises / is surprised*___ that he is not dressed
                  9

in a costume.

2 Put the words in the correct order to make expressions. Use the correct punctuation.

1. you / right / 're ___You're right.___

2. sure / are / you _____

3. I / didn't / that / oh / know _____

4. true / 's / that _____

3 Complete the conversations. Use the expressions from Activity 2.

A: Our meeting is in Room A36 at 11:30, isn't it?

B: No, it's at 10:00.

A: _____? I thought it was at 11.30.
      1

B: No, it was changed to 10:00.

A: Oh, I _____.
        2

B: Well, an e-mail was sent to everyone yesterday afternoon.

A: Let me look… Yes, _____. That's annoying. It was changed last week, too.
           3

B: _____. I guess it's always a good idea to check your e-mail before a meeting.
    4

GET CONNECTED

Avoiding media overload

People spend so much time with new media and information technology that it's easy to get distracted and overwhelmed. Information overload can weaken our decision-making abilities, cause us to make mistakes, and create stress. So what can we do to avoid media overload?

1. Don't open your e-mail every time you receive a new message. Instead, set aside specific times to check your e-mail. For example, check it once in the morning, once in the afternoon, and once or twice in the evening.

2. It's easy to check social networks every five minutes, but that makes it difficult to finish important tasks like studying for a test or doing a project for work. Don't keep your social network page open all day. Set aside certain times of day to see what your friends are doing.

3. Don't add to other people's information overload. When you write an e-mail, think twice before you click "send." Does the person that you're sending it to really need to read it? Did you click "reply all?" Does everyone on the list need to receive the e-mail?

4. For one day, keep a log of how much time you spend with media. Write down every time you check your e-mail, go online, text, or watch television. At the end of the day, add it up. You may be surprised.

5. Spend one hour each day away from all types of information technology. That includes your phone, your computer, your tablet, and even your television.

GET Started

1 Look at Jeff's information technology log on page 55. Answer the questions below.

1. How much time did Jeff spend on a social network on this day?

   _____

2. How much time did he spend e-mailing and texting?

   _____

3. How much time did he spend watching television?

   _____

4. How much time did he spend with information technology in total?

   _____

Jeff's information technology log

Time	Activity
9 AM	9:00-9:45 social network
10 AM	10:00-10:30 e-mail
	10:30-10:40 text
11 AM	
12 PM	12:00-12:20 social network (during lunch)
	12:45-1:00 text and e-mail
1 PM	
2 PM	
3 PM	3:15-4:00 online game
4 PM	
5 PM	4:00-6:00 text, e-mail (while studying)
6 PM	
7 PM	
8 PM	8:00-9:30 television
9 PM	
10 PM	9:30-11:00 text, social network, e-mail
11 PM	

GET Together

2 Work with a partner. Discuss the questions below.

1. Do you think Jeff spends too little, too much, or the right amount of time with information technology? Why?

2. What can Jeff do to limit his time with information technology?

3. Think of two more ways to avoid media overload.

GET To It!

3 Answer the questions about your own media use.

1. What kinds of information technology do you use every day? How much time do you think you spend on each kind?

2. Do you think you have information overload? Why or why not?

3. Which of the tips from page 54 can you follow to avoid or decrease information overload in your own life?

Now I can... avoid media overload.

> > > > > ☐ Not at all ☐ Well ☐ Very well

Take it online

Find the average amount of time a person in your country spends online.

A VOCABULARY: Personality

1 **Circle the word that describes the person in the picture.**

1. positive / shy

2. boring / upbeat

3. social / negative

2 **Match the questions with the two possible answers.**

_____ 1. What is she like?

_____ 2. What does she like?

a. She likes volleyball.

b. She's very dependable.

c. a little shy

d. Indian food

3 **Match the opposites.**

_____ 1. easygoing   _____ 4. boring   a. antisocial   d. uptight

_____ 2. upbeat   _____ 5. outgoing   b. shy   e. unreliable

_____ 3. social   _____ 6. dependable   c. interesting   f. negative

4 **Complete the sentences. Use the words in the box.**

boring	interesting	~~reliable~~	outgoing
upbeat	~~easygoing~~	negative	uptight

My co-worker, Nathan, is an _____*easygoing*_____ person, but he's also very _____*reliable*_____.
                                                    1   2

Our workplace is very stressful, but Nathan is always smiling and _____, which
                                                                                    3

helps a lot because there are a lot of _____ people at work. Nathan works very hard,
                                                          4

but he's not a _____ person at all. In fact, he likes doing a lot of interesting things in
                              5

his free time. He's very _____ because he likes doing a lot of fun, unusual hobbies in
                                        6

his free time. He has lots of friends, and he's so much fun at a party. He makes friends easily because

he's so _____. He always has a smile and a positive attitude, so it's difficult to feel
                    7

_____ when you see him!
          8

B GRAMMAR: Modal verbs—*might/should*

1 Complete the chart. Use the sentences in the box to complete the meaning of each statement.

It's definite.	It's possible.

	might/will	
Affirmative	We might be late.	We'll be late.
Negative	We _____ be on time.	We _____ be on time.
Meaning	_____	_____

2 Complete the sentences. Use the words in the box.

might not	~~should~~	shouldn't	might

Giving advice

1. You _____ *should* _____ wear something light at night.

   Drivers _____ see you in dark clothes.

2. You _____ drive when you're tired.

   You _____ fall asleep.

3 Match the words and then write sentences. Use *should/shouldn't* and *might/might not*.

__c__ 1. text while driving   a. it / rain

_____ 2. you / run outside in an earthquake   b. you / lose your work

_____ 3. take an umbrella   c. you / get in an accident

_____ 4. back up computer files   d. things / fall on you

_____ 5. put a coat on   e. it / not be warm outside

1. _____ You shouldn't text while driving. You might get in an accident. _____

2. _____

3. _____

4. _____

5. _____

1   Read the story. How does Hannah describe her husband and herself? Write A (Aiden) or
    H (Hannah).

_____ 1. interesting	_____ 4. outgoing	_____ 7. laid back	_____ 10. impatient
_____ 2. social	_____ 5. reliable	_____ 8. easygoing	_____ 11. fun
_____ 3. quiet	_____ 6. uptight	_____ 9. upbeat	_____ 12. shy

An outgoing husband

What's my husband, Aiden, like? Well, he's an interesting person.
He's very social—not shy at all! In fact, when we go to parties, he always
makes a big entrance so that everyone sees us! He's also one of those
people who laughs really loudly at things. I'm a pretty quiet person and
not as outgoing, so that can be embarrassing at times. I'm a little shy.
Aiden knows a lot of people and he makes friends easily. However, he
can never remember people's names. I'm much more reliable in that way. I can always
remember names and faces. We're a good team that way!

One thing about Aiden is that he likes to be in control of everything, and I know that
some people think he's uptight. They're probably right, but I wouldn't say that to anyone.
He's lucky that he has such a laid back and easygoing wife! No one would call Aiden a
very easygoing person. On the other hand, he's usually upbeat, at least with me and the
kids. That's important, even if he isn't always that way at work.

There are a few things I find annoying. He can be a little impatient with people. He
interrupts people a lot, and he isn't a good listener. But, again, that's OK with me because,
as I said, I'm pretty quiet. But Aiden's usually fun to be with, and we get along great. We
make a good team, and that's what's most important.

2   Mark each statement about Aiden true (T) or false (F).

_____ 1. He makes a lot of noise when he enters a party so people will look at him.

_____ 2. He smiles quietly when something amuses him.

_____ 3. He makes friends easily.

_____ 4. He always remembers names and faces.

_____ 5. He often interrupts people.

3   Answer the questions about you.

1. Are you a quiet person or an outgoing person?

2. Are you a positive person or a negative person most of the time?

3. Do you always remember faces and names of the people you meet?

4. Do you make friends easily or more gradually?

5. Are you easygoing, or do you like to be in control?

D EVERYDAY EXPRESSIONS: Comparing experiences

1 Complete the expressions. Use the words in the box.

do (x2)	me, too (x2)	know what you mean	am

First person's statement	Second person's reply	Third person's reply
I am sick today.	So _____ I.	Oh, _____.
I don't like pineapple.	Neither _____ I.	I _____.
I play basketball.	So _____ I.	_____.

2 Match the statements with the two possible replies.

1. I can play the guitar. _____b, d_____
2. I can't swim. _____
3. We didn't enjoy the play. _____
4. I'm American. _____

a. Neither can I.
b. Oh, I can't.
c. I can.
d. So can I.

e. So am I.
f. I know what you mean.
g. Me, too.
h. Neither did we.

3 Write the response of someone with the same experience, then of someone with a different experience.

1. I've been to Argentina. **A:** _____So have I_____. **B:** _____I haven't_____.

2. I don't like cold weather. **A:** _____. **B:** _____.

3. I won't be here next week. **A:** _____. **B:** _____.

4. I work in a bank. **A:** _____. **B:** _____.

5. I'm going swimming today. **A:** _____. **B:** _____.

6. I can't speak Russian. **A:** _____. **B:** _____.

7. I didn't go out last weekend. **A:** _____. **B:** _____.

8. I slept well last night. **A:** _____. **B:** _____.

4 Write your own response to the statements.

1. I don't work in an office. _____Neither do I. OR I do._____.
2. I need a vacation. _____.
3. I can play a musical instrument. _____.
4. I had coffee for breakfast. _____.
5. I don't have any brothers and sisters. _____.
6. I'd like to go scuba diving. _____.
7. I'm a shy person. _____.
8. I didn't go shopping yesterday. _____.

UNIT 14 Here comes the bride.

A VOCABULARY: Getting married

1 Complete the crossword.

Across

4. the clothes that the bride wears

6. the flowers that the bride carries

7. jewelry worn on a finger

8. At a wedding, the bride and groom get _____ .

Down

1. the woman who is getting married

2. usually the groom's best friend or brother

3. the man who is getting married

5. the people who are invited to the wedding

6. these women help the bride

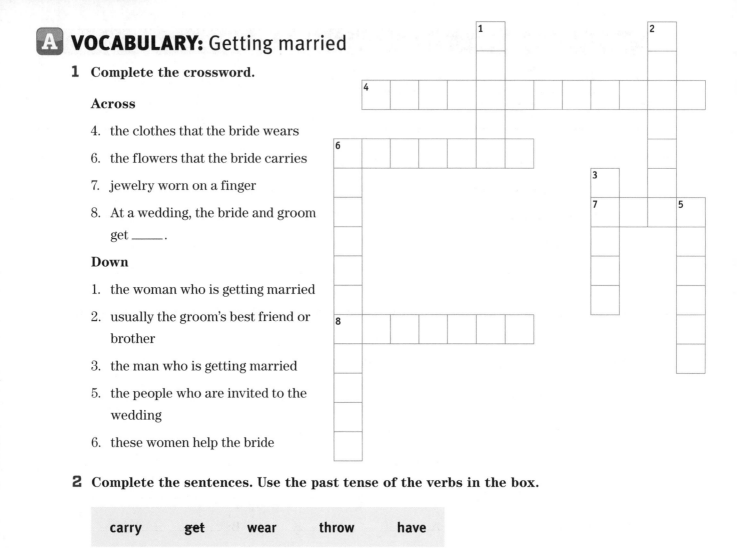

2 Complete the sentences. Use the past tense of the verbs in the box.

carry	~~get~~	wear	throw	have

1. My cousin _____*got*_____ married last weekend.

2. They _____ the wedding on a beach in front of a hotel.

3. The guests _____ rice and confetti.

4. The bride _____ a beautiful bouquet.

5. She _____ a yellow wedding dress.

3 Think about the last wedding you went to. Answer these questions.

1. What color dress did the bride wear? _____

2. Where was the wedding? _____

3. Were there any bridesmaids? If so, how many were there? _____

4. Where was the reception? _____

5. Did the couple go on a honeymoon? If so, where? _____

B GRAMMAR: Direct and indirect objects

1 Complete the chart. Use the words in the box.

Indirect object	~~Subject~~	Verb	Direct object

Direct and indirect objects			
Subject			
Austin	sent	an e-mail	to his boss.
Alicia	gave	a book	to her boyfriend.

2 What's happening in the pictures? Complete the sentences. Use the present continuous and the words in the box.

some money	Max	~~his friend~~	the manager
her daughter	a letter	~~the car~~	a report

1. He _is selling the car to his friend_ . (sell)

2. He _____ . (mail)

3. She _____ . (e-mail)

4. She _____ . (give)

3 Put the words in the correct order. Then circle the indirect object.

1. I _sent a card to my parents_ . (to / my / parents / sent / a / card)

2. I _____ . (my / parents / sent / a / card)

3. You _____ . (that / picture / gave / to / us)

4. You _____ . (that / picture / gave / us)

4 Rewrite the sentences in Activity 2 without *to*.

1. _____ He's selling his friend the car _____ .

2. _____ .

3. _____ .

4. _____ .

C READING AND WRITING: Traditions

Giving gifts in Japan

In Japan, people often give gifts. There are a lot of traditions associated with giving gifts, and it's very useful for visitors to know about them.

It's traditional to offer a gift when you meet someone for the first time. A gift means that you hope for a long and successful relationship. A gift should match the status of the person that you are giving it to. So you should give a more expensive gift to a more important person. But be careful. A very expensive gift can be embarrassing for the receiver.

In fact, the gift itself is not the most important thing. The gift symbolizes your respect for the other person. The way that you give the gift is much more important than the gift itself. For example, your gift should be in a beautiful box or wrapped in nice paper. Shops in Japan will always wrap gifts for you. When you give the gift, you should offer it with both hands. As you offer it, you should bow slightly to show that you're offering a small gift as a symbol of your respect.

When somebody offers you a gift in Japan, it's polite to refuse it once or twice. People don't usually accept a gift immediately. Also, you shouldn't open it in front of the person who has given it to you. You should accept it, say thank you, and then put it to one side to open later.

What things should or shouldn't you give? Food, such as chocolates or cookies, is always a good idea. A gift with two things in it is lucky, but don't give anything with four, nine, or thirteen things. These are unlucky numbers. You should also avoid giving anything red, as this color is associated with funerals.

1 Which of these should you do in Japan? Check (✓) the good ideas and put an X (✗) next to the bad ideas.

- [ ] 1. Exchange gifts at your first meeting.
- [ ] 2. Bow when you give a gift.
- [ ] 3. Make sure the wrapping is beautiful.
- [ ] 4. Say thank you when recieving a gift.
- [ ] 5. Refuse a gift that is offered to you once.
- [ ] 6. Offer a gift with one hand.
- [ ] 7. Immediately open a gift that you receive.
- [ ] 8. Give something that's red.

2 What gift–giving traditions are there in your country? Complete the text.

In _____₁ people usually give people gifts _____₂.
They usually give _____₃. When you give a gift, you should /
shouldn't _____₄. When you receive a gift, you should / shouldn't
_____₅. A good gift to buy is _____₆, but you shouldn't give
_____₇ because _____₈.

D EVERYDAY EXPRESSIONS: Discussing possibilities

1 Read the story. <u>Underline</u> the eight mistakes.

The <u>Chief Executive</u> wants to see Lucy. Russell suggests that maybe she wants to promote her. Lucy says it's more likely that she's going to give her more hours. Lucy says that whatever it is, she'll find out at 2:30. Later, Lucy tells Russell that she has won the Personal Assistant of the Month award. She says she was very worried when she heard the news. There's going to be a celebration at work the next day when she gets presented with a prize and certificate. The prize is lunch for four at a good restaurant. Lucy's mother is going to go with her. The meal's scheduled for the next day.

2 Rewrite the summary correctly.

<u>The boss wants to see Lucy.</u> _____

_____

_____

_____

_____

3 Complete the expressions.

1. What's it _____?

2. It's more _____ that...

3. I have no _____.

4. I hope you're _____.

4 Complete the conversations. Use the expressions in Activity 3.

1. **A:** The boss says she wants to see you.

   B: What's _____$_1$?

   A: I _____$_2$.

   B: Maybe she's going to offer me more money.

   A: Maybe, but it's _____$_3$ that she's going to fire you. You were late again yesterday.

   B: Well, I _____$_4$.

2. **A:** Do you think the builders will finish this week?

   B: Possibly. But it's _____$_1$ that they'll still be here next week.

   A: I _____$_2$, because I'm getting tired of all the noise and dust.

   B: By the way, did you see the note in the break room?

   A: No, what's _____$_2$?

   B: I _____$_2$. I couldn't understand it.

UNIT 15 Lights, camera, action!

A VOCABULARY: Movies

1 Circle the kinds of movies in the wordsnake.

garomancedsdramayactionmohorrorlecomedynewscience-fictionly

2 Complete the sentences. Use the words in the box.

comedy	romance	horror
dramas	science-fiction	action

1. The best cure for stress is laughter. That's why I always try to find a good _____ to watch when I'm feeling stressed.

2. Cheri's boyfriend is fascinated by space and space travel. His favorite movies are all _____. He especially likes *Star Wars* and *Star Trek*.

3. Josiah is one of those unusual men who isn't afraid to say that he loves a good _____, especially on a date.

4. Shana can't be scared enough! She loves getting scared by good _____ movies like *Halloween*.

5. Bruce Lee made martial arts like Kung Fu very popular in _____ movies.

6. A lot of doctors and lawyers say they don't want to watch medical or courtroom _____ in their free time. They remind them too much of their work.

3 Answer the questions about you.

1. What kind of movie do you watch after a hard week at work/school? _____

2. What kind of movie do you watch when you are feeling sad? _____

3. What kind of movie do you like to watch with your friends? _____

4. What kind of movie is a good date night movie for you? _____

5. What kinds of movies are the most popular in your country? _____

6. What kinds of movies do you think are the most expensive to make? _____

7. Imagine you are an actor or movie director. What kind of movie do you want to make? Why?

_____

_____

B GRAMMAR: Modal verbs—can/must/have to/be able to

1 Complete the chart.

can/can't		
	Affirmative	**Negative**
Past	I could drive, so I did.	I _____ drive, so my friend did.
Present	I _____ drive.	I can't drive.
Future	I'll be able to drive.	I _____ drive.

must/have to		
Past	You had to go.	You _____ go.
Present	You must go. You have to go.	You don't have to go.
Future	You _____ go.	You _____ go.

2 Addie has broken her foot. What *will* or *won't* she be able to do? Complete the sentences.

1. She ___won't be able to___ go swimming.

2. She _____ use a computer.

3. She _____ go jogging.

4. She _____ play the piano.

5. She _____ go to the movies.

6. She _____ drive a car.

3 Complete the sentences with *can, can't, must, had to,* or *didn't have to.*

1. If everyone else is busy, I ___can___ cook dinner tonight.

2. I _____ make an important decision last night, so I did.

3. Her cell phone is broken. She _____ buy a new one today.

4. Nicky _____ go to work yesterday, even though it was Monday.

5. I _____ get up early when I go to sleep very late.

4 Read the sentences. Write about the people. Use *'ll have to* or *won't have to* and the words in the box.

go shopping	~~stand up~~	pay by credit card
drive to work	share an office	

1. All the seats on the train are taken. We ___'ll have to stand up___ .

2. Carson doesn't have any cash. He _____ .

3. Aubrey has been promoted. She _____ .

4. It's Sunday tomorrow. Luis and Maria _____ .

5. There's no food in the refrigerator. We _____ .

1   **Read about Lewis. Answer the questions below.**

I Love Movies

I usually go to the movies every week. I used to go more often because I used to write movie reviews for the local newspaper. I had to go and see all the latest movies. I really enjoyed that because I could watch lots of movies, but I didn't have to pay for them. However, I changed jobs two years ago, and after that I couldn't find the time to do the reviews anymore.

I still like going to the movies because I prefer seeing movies on a big screen. I usually just watch movies at home, though—either on DVDs, streamed from the Internet, or just on TV. My TV has over 20 movie channels, so there's always something to watch. In fact, there's usually too much to watch. It's almost impossible to decide what to watch some evenings.

I like most kinds of movies, but there are definitely some I like more than others. I don't usually watch romances or musicals. I like action movies a lot, like martial arts movies or spy adventures. I watch a lot of comedies, too. But my all-time favorites are science-fiction movies. I love all the great special effects. The best movie that I've ever seen is *Alien*. I know it's old, but I just love it. Even though I've watched it more than ten times, I still get scared. I like some of the famous Chinese movies, too, like *Hero* and *The House of Flying Daggers*.

1. Why did Lewis used to go to the movies a lot?

2. What kinds of movies does Lewis usually watch?

3. What's the best movie he's ever seen?

4. What kinds of movies does Lewis mention?

5. What are the two movie types from page 64 that Lewis doesn't mention?

6. What kind of movies does he like the most?

2   **Mark the statements true (T) or false (F).**

_____ 1. He goes to the movies once a month.

_____ 2. He used to write reviews for a radio station.

_____ 3. He got a new job two years ago.

_____ 4. He streams all his movies from the Internet.

_____ 5. He likes the movies because he goes with his friends.

_____ 6. He likes science-fiction movies because of the special effects.

_____ 7. He's seen *Alien* three times.

_____ 8. *Hero* is a Chinese movie.

D EVERYDAY EXPRESSIONS: Bad luck

1 Number the parts of the story in the correct order.

_____ a. Peter asks Jordan about his luck getting work.

_____ b. Sarah reassures Peter by telling him that her parents like him a lot.

_____ c. Peter leaves to meet Sarah and her parents at an art museum even though he doesn't particularly like going to art museums.

_____ d. Peter meets Jordan in the park and they talk about what happened at dinner with Sarah's parents.

___1___ e. Peter tells Sarah he's worried about the impression he's making on her parents.

_____ f. Sarah explains that her parents can see how much Peter likes her.

_____ g. Jordan explains that he has an audition. It's the weekend of the dinner with Lucy, but he explains that he has to do the audition anyway.

2 Find the mistakes. Rewrite the expressions correctly.

1. I can't seem to do nothing right _____

2. I've made a food of myself _____

3. I messed things up against _____

4. It's trouble timing _____

3 Complete the sentences with the correct expressions from Activity 2.

1. Peter feels like he just _____ around Sarah's parents.

2. Peter tells Jordan he _____ again at the dinner party.

3. He thinks he's _____ the last two times.

4. Peter tells Jordan that _____ because it's a really good role.

4 Choose the correct sentences.

1. a. Oh, no. I've done another mistake.

   b. Oh, no. I've made another mistake.

2. a. I'm not making anything tonight. Should we go out?

   b. I'm not doing anything tonight. Should we go out?

3. a. I'm afraid I won't be able to fix the computer.

   b. I'm afraid I won't can fix the computer.

4. a. We didn't must pay for the meal.

   b. We didn't have to pay for the meal.

A VOCABULARY: At college

1 Complete the story. Use the words in the box.

lecture	undergraduate	professor
assignment	degree	student
seminar	notes	diplomas
on campus	graduating	graduation ceremony

My name's Hailey, and I'm a _____ at Hudson University.
                                    1

I'm an _____ and I'm studying for a _____ in Biology. In this picture,
          2   3

the students are attending a _____ . The _____ is giving the lecture
                                4   5

and the students are taking _____ . At the end, the professor will give the students an
                                6

_____ and a reading list. The students will have a _____ in a few days,
        7   8

and they'll discuss the assignment.

There are a lot of parents _____ today. They're here for
                                9

a _____ . The students who have finished their programs are
      10

_____ today. They'll get their _____ at
      11   12

the ceremony.

2 Circle the correct words.

1. I'm *studying for / noting* a degree in Psychology.

2. I *attend / sit* two or three lectures a day.

3. We're *taking / making* a test next week.

4. I have two assignments to *make / do* this week.

5. I'm working hard to *fail / pass* my tests.

6. I *took / did* a lot of notes in the lecture.

3 Complete the paragraph about you. Circle the correct words and complete the sentences.

I *was / am* a student at _____ . I *studied / am studying* for a *degree*

/ diploma in _____ . It *was / is* a _____ year course.

I *took / will take* my final exams in _____ . I *received / will receive* my

_____ at a graduation ceremony in _____ .

B GRAMMAR: Present perfect continuous

1 Complete the chart. Use the words in the box for the columns on the left. Use the *-ing* forms of the verbs in parentheses for the column on the right.

has	haven't	been	hasn't	have

Present perfect continuous			
I You We They	_____ 've have not _____	_____	_____ TV. (watch)
He She It	_____ 's has not		_____ a computer. (use) _____ . (run)

2 Complete the sentences. Use the present perfect continuous form of the verbs in parentheses.

1. We _____ here since 2010. (live)

2. She _____ English for three years. (study)

3. I _____ hard today. (work)

4. Nate _____ all afternoon. (swim)

3 Match the sentences with the correct pictures.

_____ 1. I've been reading this book for an hour.
  (present perfect continuous)

_____ 2. I've read that book.
  (present perfect)

a.   b.

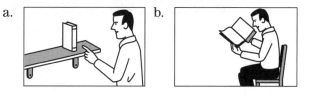

4 Circle the correct words.

1. I've *answered / been answering* e-mails all afternoon, and there are still 20 more.

2. Tim has *fixed / been fixing* the car, so we can get in and go now.

3. I've *done / been doing* my assignment, so I'm going to hand it in to the professor now.

4. I've *sat / been sitting* in this traffic jam for two hours and we still aren't moving.

5. I've *written / been writing* all the letters, so I can go home now.

6. The man has *repaired / been repairing* the machine for an hour, but it still isn't working.

7. Are we there yet? We've *walked / been walking* for three hours.

8. Peyton's *taken / been taking* five exams this week, but he's finished now.

C READING: Applying for jobs

1 Read the letter. Choose the correct prepositions to complete it.

Human Resources Manager at Freeway Magazines
15 State Street
Davis, CA 91022

Alexis Wells
26 Alta Vista Avenue
Santa Barbara, CA 93711

Dear Ms. Andrews,

I would like to apply __*for / to*__ the position __*from / of*__ Publicity Manager with Freeway Magazines. As you can see from my resume, I have a degree __*on / in*__ psychology from Madison University. As part of my program at Madison, I had an internship for six months __*with / for*__ a computer company.

After I graduated, I started to work __*with / for*__ Face-to-Face Advertising. I worked there for two years in their Market Research department. For the last six years, I've been working __*on / for*__ Multimedia Solutions. I started as the Assistant Manager in the Marketing department, where I was responsible __*to / for*__ advertising. After three years, I was promoted __*at / to*__ the position of Manager and I am now __*at / in*__ charge of a department of five people.

In addition __*on / to*__ my degree, I have a certificate __*with / in*__ marketing. I have also taken classes __*at / in*__ publicity and finance.

I have really enjoyed my work with Multimedia Solutions, but I'm now looking for a new challenge __*in / on*__ a larger company. I believe that my qualifications and experience are right __*from / for*__ the position of Publicity Manager with your company. I look forward __*to / in*__ hearing from you.

Best regards,
Alexis Wells

2 Complete the Human Resources Manager's notes.

Name: _____

Main qualification(s): a _____ in _____ from _____

	Work experience: where?	Position / Duties?	How long?
1.	a _____ company in _____	an _____	_____
2.	Face-to-Face _____	worked in _____	_____
3.	_____ Solutions	Assistant _____ in _____; responsible _____	3 years
4.	Multimedia _____	_____; in charge _____	_____

Other qualifications:

Reason for applying:

D EVERYDAY EXPRESSIONS: Responding to news

1 Complete the summary. Use the words in the box.

the news	his audition time	Jordan	break up with him
told her yet	Sarah	Lucy	see
cancels at the last minute	on the dinner date	Cozy Cup	doesn't give him a chance

Sarah hears from Peter that Jordan can't go

_____ with Lucy. She comes into

1

_____ and sees _____ there. Sarah

2   3

tells her _____. Lucy is upset for

4

different reasons; because Jordan always _____,

5

and because he hadn't _____. Later, _____ comes into

6   7

Cozy Cup looking for Lucy, but he doesn't _____ her at first. He asks _____

8   9

if she knows where Lucy is. He explains that he's changed _____ so he will

10

be able to go to dinner with Lucy. When Lucy sees Jordan, she _____ to

11

explain. Instead she tells him that she wants to _____.

12

2 Complete the expressions. Use the words in the box.

news	terrible	heard	no

1. I just _____ the news.

2. Oh, _____.

3. That's _____ news!

4. That's wonderful _____!

3 Complete the conversations. Use the expressions in Activity 2.

1. **A:** Guess what. I've been promoted.

   B: _____!

1

2. **A:** Why are you looking so sad?

   B: I _____ that Zoe and Wyatt are splitting up.

2

   A: Really? _____ news!

3

3. **A:** I _____ that Gabriella's aunt has died.

4

   B: Oh, _____. That's _____!

5   6

GET CONNECTED

Using collaboration software

File sharing or collaboration software, like Google Docs and Webex, allows people to work together on a project. Users can all look at the same document, photo, video, or slideshow and edit it together.

To use collaboration software, a user uploads something online that he or she wants to share and invites people to view it. Everyone can then work on it at the same time. This can be useful for students or co-workers who are working on a project together but cannot meet in person.

Using file sharing software means that you don't have to e-mail documents or photos, edit them, and send them back and forth. Sending documents back and forth takes a long time and can be confusing. File sharing software makes working on the same document faster and easier. With many of these programs, users can see who is making changes and what changes they are making, and they can communicate with each other by chatting through the software.

GET Started

1 Look at the file sharing website on page 73. Answer the questions below.

1. Who shared the document?

   _____

2. How many people are viewing the document?

   _____

3. How many people are working on the project?

   _____

2 Look again at the website. Complete each sentence with the correct name.

1. _____ is correcting grammar.

2. _____ is adding information to the document.

3. _____ is not viewing the document.

> > > >

File | Edit | Insert | Format | Help

Doc Share Plus

Project Update
Communications 101, Professor Herbert
Team Members: John Lee, Erin Jenner, Tina Marks,
Ken Kubota, Luis Bayon

We've been worki[Ken] on our report on the history of social networking. So far, we have researched information online, and we've read several articles about Facebook, Twitter, YouTube, and other sim[Erin]. We have called the Facebook offices to ask for an interview with one of the employees. We left a message, but they haven't called us back yet.

John L and three others are viewing.

- John L
- Ken K
- Erin J
- Luis B

John L has shared a document.

John L: Hi, guys. I wrote a draft of our update. What do you think?

Ken K: It looks good. I think it should say, "We've been working," and not, "We've been work."

Erin J: Yes, that's right. Also, let's say, "YouTube, and other similar websites," or something like that.

Luis B: That's a good idea.

GET Together

GET To It!

3 Work with a partner. How do you think you could use collaboration software for work or for school? Make a list of ideas.

4 What are some possible advantages and disadvantages of using collaboration software on a project like the one above? Complete the chart. Then discuss your chart with a group.

Advantages (+)	Disadvantages (-)

> > > > > **Now I can...** use collaboration software.

☐ Not at all ☐ Well ☐ Very well

Take it online
Find two more examples of collaboration software.

Self-Study Listening

GO ONLINE Go to www.oxfordlearn.com/login to download the audio for Workbook 3.

UNIT 1: Let's introduce ourselves.

1 **Listen to the introductions. Fill in the forms with the correct information.**

1.

Name: _____Roberto Fonesca_____

Country: _____

Age: _____

Occupation: _____

Employer: _____

Relationship or Marital status:

Single Engaged Married Divorced Widowed

Interests and/or hobbies:

_____

2.

Name: _____Julia Philips_____

Home: _____

Age: _____

Occupation: _____

Employer: _____

Relationship or Marital status:

Single Engaged Married Divorced Widowed

Interests and/or hobbies:

_____

2 **Listen again. Mark the statements true (T) or false (F).**

_____ 1. Roberto is probably creative.

_____ 2. Roberto is looking for a new girlfriend.

_____ 3. Roberto likes to stay home on weekends.

_____ 4. Julia probably likes to cook.

_____ 5. Julia doesn't like computers.

_____ 6. Julia wants to date again.

UNIT 2: Things happen.

1 **Listen. Match the items with the names.**

_____ 1. Greg   a. a laptop

_____ 2. Eduardo   b. car keys

_____ 3. Diana   c. a motorcycle

_____ 4. Olivia   d. money

_____ 5. Joshua   e. a cup of coffee

2 **Listen again. Answer the questions.**

1. How did they find out whose laptop it is? _____.

2. What kind of car does Phil drive?   _____.

3. Where does Olivia work?   _____.

4. Who is Joshua's girlfriend?   _____.

5. How much money is it?   _____.

UNIT 3: Buildings everywhere!

1 Listen. Number the homes in the order you hear them.

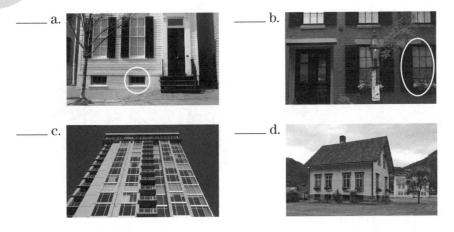

_____ a.

_____ b.

_____ c.

_____ d.

2 Listen again. Write the correct letter. There can be more than one.

_____ 1. Which home is owned by the speaker's parents?

_____ 2. Which home is dark?

_____ 3. Which home is rented?

_____ 4. Which homes are convenient?

_____ 5. Which home is cheap?

_____ 6. Which homes are quiet?

_____ 7. Which home has spacious and light rooms?

UNIT 4: Seeing old friends

1 Listen to Gabe and Claire talk about their lives. Who did what? Write G (Gabe) or C (Claire) next to each item.

_____ 1. worked as a teacher's assistant.

_____ 2. studied Spanish in Spain.

_____ 3. worked on a farm in Ecuador.

_____ 4. lived with a family.

_____ 5. taught English in Argentina.

_____ 6. traveled in India.

_____ 7. hiked in the mountains in Nepal.

_____ 8. went to graduate school to get a Masters.

_____ 9. got a job in Washington, D.C.

_____ 10. got an English teaching job at a community college.

2 Listen again. Answer the questions.

1. Why did Gabe stop teaching high school? _____.

2. Where is Molly from? _____.

3. Why did Claire return to the U.S.? _____.

4. Where does she want to stay? _____.

UNIT 5: Congratulations!

1 Listen to the radio interviews. What do the people do? Match each interview with the correct achievement.

_____ 1. Avery   _____ 2. Evan   _____ 3. Autumn

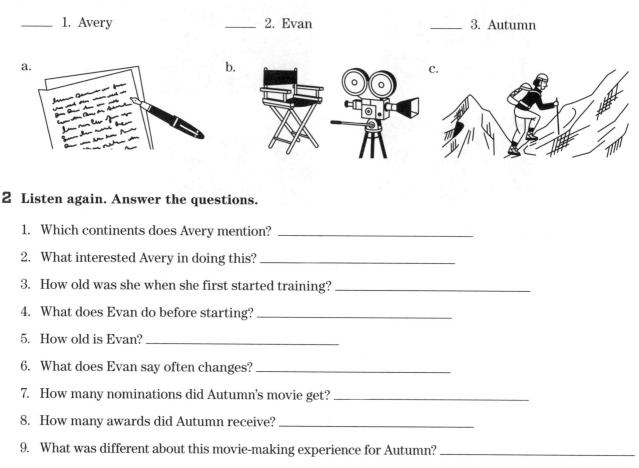

a.   b.   c.

2 Listen again. Answer the questions.

1. Which continents does Avery mention? _____

2. What interested Avery in doing this? _____

3. How old was she when she first started training? _____

4. What does Evan do before starting? _____

5. How old is Evan? _____

6. What does Evan say often changes? _____

7. How many nominations did Autumn's movie get? _____

8. How many awards did Autumn receive? _____

9. What was different about this movie-making experience for Autumn? _____

UNIT 6: Healthy living

1 Listen to Katrina and Richard. Why does each one exercise and eat a healthy diet? Write K (Katrina) or R (Richard) next to the correct reasons.

_____ 1. to lose weight   _____ 3. to manage stress

_____ 2. to prevent another heart attack   _____ 4. to feel great

2 Listen again. Make notes in the boxes to complete the chart.

	Indoor Exercise	Outdoor Exercise	Diet Changes	Other lifestyle changes	Still needs to lose weight: Yes or No?
Katrina					
Richard					

UNIT 7: What a Pain!

 1 Listen. Put the events in order.

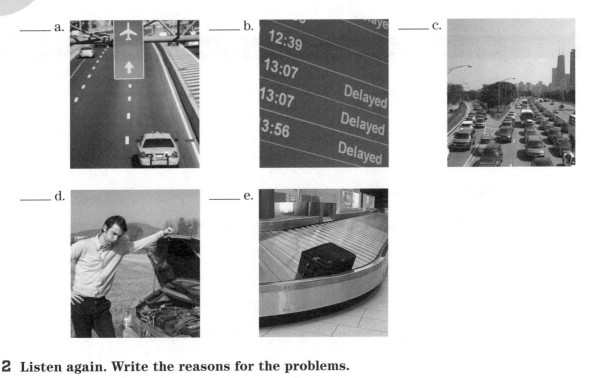

_____ a.   _____ b.   _____ c.

_____ d.   _____ e.

 2 Listen again. Write the reasons for the problems.

1. The car broke down because _____.

2. The flight was delayed because _____.

3. Alyssa and Jonah stayed an extra hour at the airport because _____.

4. They're stuck in traffic because _____.

UNIT 8: Eat Up!

🔊 **1 Listen. Complete the chart.**

Food	Description
1. steak	medium-rare
2.	
3.	
4.	
5.	
6.	

🔊 **2 Listen again. Circle the numbers of the conversations that take place in a restaurant.**

Conversations: 1   2   3   4   5   6

UNIT 9: What a Disaster!

1 Listen to the news reports. Complete the chart with checks (✓) for disasters that are happening in each area and X's (✗) for disasters that are not.

	earthquakes	tsunamis	hurricanes	floods	forest fires	droughts
Central Africa						
Florida						
Malaysia						

2 Listen again. Mark the statements true (T) or false (F).

_____ 1. The people in Central Africa are suffering because there isn't enough food and water.

_____ 2. The United Nations has not started providing aid to Central Africa.

_____ 3. It is winter in Central Florida at the moment.

_____ 4. One million people are without power in Florida.

_____ 5. The amount of deaths in central Malaysia is low because many people were outside when the disaster hit.

_____ 6. Previous rains are preventing forest fires from happening in central Malaysia.

UNIT 10: I used To...

1 Listen. Put a number on the people in the picture who are doing the jobs Martin used to do. Number the people in order.

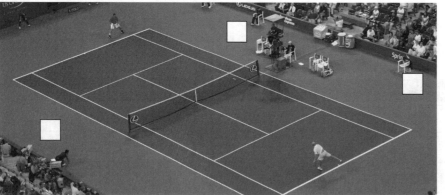

1. _____

2. _____

3. _____

2 Listen again. Check (✓) the things Martin says he used to do.

_____ 1. live in Florida

_____ 2. play tennis

_____ 3. watch the tennis players

_____ 4. chase balls for the players

_____ 5. get tips from the players

_____ 6 work as a lines person

_____ 7. prefer being a lines person

_____ 8. play tennis at college

_____ 9. be a tennis umpire for the college matches

_____ 10. get yelled at by the players